The
Classic Guide
to
SAILING

The
Classic Guide
to
SAILING

E. F. KNIGHT

AMBERLEY

Originally published in 1902
This edition first published 2014

Amberley Publishing
The Hill, Stroud, Gloucestershire, GL5 4EP
www.amberley-books.com

Copyright © Amberley Publishing, 2014

ISBN 978 1 4456 4214 7 (print)
ISBN 978 1 4456 4216 1 (ebook)

British Library Cataloguing in Publication Data.
A catalogue record for this book is available from the British Library.

Typesetting by Amberley Publishing.
Printed in Great Britain.

Contents

Introduction

Throughout human history, sailing has been integral in the growth of civilization, whether it be for trade, transport or, perhaps more importantly over the last century, for warfare. The very first boats are presumed to have been dugout canoes, and one hypothesis states that the earliest seaworthy boats may have been developed up to 45,000 years ago. The earliest known depiction of a ship in sail can be found in Kuwait from around 5000 BC, and the Ancient Egyptians certainly had knowledge of sail construction, according to Herodotus. The technology of boat building and sailing developed from the Middle Ages to the present day, as explorers attempted ever longer voyages into more extreme conditions, requiring improvements to sails, rigging, masts and hulls. The period from the fifteenth to the seventeenth century was known as the Age of Discovery, and European ships travelled the world in search of alternative trade routes, to discover new lands, and to establish new colonies.

The advent of the Age of Steam in the 1800s slowly put an end to the Age of the Sail, and in the twentieth century the internal combustion engine, gas turbine and nuclear marine propulsion have far outstripped the capabilities of the sailing boat. However, recreational sailing and racing are worldwide pursuits in the modern day, and have become multi-billion-pound industries. The spirit of adventure is, likewise, still alive and well in the form of passagemaking.

Edward Frederick Knight was an English barrister, soldier and, most importantly, a journalist. He was one of the great adventurers of the nineteenth century, sailing to Trinidade off the coast of Brazil in search of treasure. As a journalist, Edward laid down much of his accumulated knowledge and expertise in a book entitled *Small Boat Sailing*, one of the very first manuals of the craft. This was a strong influence on Arthur Ransome, who used the book to teach himself how to sail. *The Classic Guide to Sailing* is a remastered version of this seminal work. It includes many contemporary sketches and illustrations, and instructs the budding sailor in how to become a true master of the sailing boat.

The Editor

1

The Selection of a Boat

This work is intended for the use of the tyro who has little or no experience of sailing – not for the owner of the luxurious floating palace, but for the young Englishman who has a true love of the sea, and who, though unable to undertake long cruises on a smart schooner, or to race his cutter against the crack ships of the season, is yet ambitious to own and to sail single-handed his small craft, ready to rough it in the pursuit of his favourite pastime. Without doubt he who sails his own little vessel appreciates best all pleasures of yachting. 'The smaller the vessel, the better the sport,' has long been a maxim of mine. I have sailed my own vessels, from the tiniest craft up to seventy-tonners, upon many seas; but I think that in this particular sport I have got the most unadulterated delight out of the open boats of my boyhood, and out of my first five-tonner, a little yawl with which I cruised single-handed, or sometimes with one friend on board, for thousands of miles along the shores of several European countries, visiting out-of-the-way creeks, remote islets (as on the Baltic) inhabited by primitive folk, fishing havens, shallow estuaries and straits, and winding fjords, inaccessible to larger yachts, which have to make their passages from one well-known great seaport to another, missing the most interesting features of the coasts by which they sail.

And how the single-handed sailor comes to love his little vessel! He takes such a keen pride in keeping her smart without the assistance of others, and he is indeed jealous of their interference. Those who know not the delights of small-boat sailing sometimes dub the amusement a monotonous one; and, occasionally, it may certainly appear to be so to the ignorant spectator – much as golf does, for the matter of that, to the uninitiated. But there is no monotony for the true sailor alone with his yacht. Loving his craft, he does not find the time hangs heavy, even when she floats idly in a calm – a position trying to the temper of those who are not enthusiasts of the sea. There is always some work to be done on board, repairs, painting, and so forth – a labour of love that he accomplishes with affectionate thoroughness; and when that is complex he awaits the wind patiently, contemplating his vessel over his pipe, admiring her, and thinking how he can do this or that to improve her; or he plans fresh cruises; or calls up pleasant memories of former cruises in her – of how at one time she showed a clean pair of heels to a craft double her size, and how she weathered that gale in the North Sea in such a year, when she behaved so well, and breasted with safety the steep seas by which bigger vessels might have been overwhelmed. No girl over her doll can contrive to make herself more perfectly happy than is the true yachtsman over his little ship.

As this book is intended for the instruction of the amateur skipper who would command his own small craft – and in most cases would be skipper, crew, and cook in one – I shall have nothing to say of the larger type of pleasure-craft, but will confine myself to dealing with small boats of various sizes, from the tiniest up-river dinghy to the ten-ton cutter or yawl. Professional sailors often declare that no book can assist a man in the acquisition of seamanship. I hold that books are of far more service than these mariners imagine, and enable the novice to acquire the elements of the art of sailing far more rapidly than would be possible otherwise. I remember well that I picked up many a wrinkle from books when I first took to sailing. But, of course, only long practice on board a craft can teach that self-confidence, that instinctive readiness to do the right thing promptly in any sudden emergency, without which all book-acquired theory is valueless at sea.

The selection of a boat is the subject of my opening chapter. Now, it is an exceedingly difficult matter to select a boat for another man. An old sailor once truly remarked that he would as soon trust a friend to choose a wife for him as to select his craft. Each man has his own taste in the matter of wives and boats. None save himself knows what will suit him best. All one can do is to proffer him some advice as to the selection of his vessel, give him some hints which are the fruit of personal experience, and then let him choose for himself.

As the novice, whether acting on the advice of friends or on his own responsibility, is almost certain to be dissatisfied with the first craft he may happen to possess, it is well that in the first instance he should purchase a cheap boat, so that when the inevitable divorce ensues the sacrifice may be the smaller. A small, stiff, open or half-decked boat snugly rigged will suit him best in the early days of his apprenticeship; but of what type that boat should be depends not only on his own idiosyncrasies but on a variety of circumstances – the character of the waters he purposes to navigate; whether his boat is to be kept on the banks of some smooth river or tideless lake, or on the shore of the restless sea; whether the water allows of the use of a deep-keel boat, or whether it be so shallow that he is compelled to employ a craft of light draft; whether he has a snug haven for his boat, or whether she has to be run through the breakers and beached on an exposed coast after each sail; and so forth.

I will suppose that the tyro has come to a decision as to the class of craft he requires, whether it be sailing dinghy or five-ton cutter, and that he is looking round the various boat-builders' yards to pick up a good second-hand craft; for it is generally a mistake to have a boat built for one until one has gained considerable experience and understands exactly what one wants. Excellent second-hand boats can often be purchased at less than a quarter of what they cost to build, and yet be in all respects practically as good as new.

But great caution should be observed in the selection. Do not be deceived by a fair exterior, so easily produced by a discriminate application of paint, putty, and oakum. Examine the vessel carefully before concluding the purchase, or you may find yourself woefully deceived. I remember, some years ago, seeing a 'great bargain' lying off the Mall, at Hammersmith – an unlikely place for a yacht. She was a cutter, of about ten tons, that had been purchased below bridges for a ridiculously small sum, by a young man of Hammersmith, who had no experience whatever of sailing, and scarcely knew one end of a boat from the other; but it was his ambition to become a yachtsman. Having bought his cutter, he had her towed up to Hammersmith, where she was to be fitted out. He modestly announced that as soon as she was ready for sea, he would take a trial trip in her across the Bay of Biscay to Spain – a bold first venture for the amateur. He invited the author to accompany him, but the latter could not see his way to avail himself of this kind offer. He would take no advice save from a man professing to be a boat-builder, who was ignorant of his work, but who set himself in a very leisurely fashion to patch the old craft up and make a good profit out of this callow youth. For months the work of preparation went on. The hull of the yacht was beautiful to the eye with glossy black paint and gold streak (concealing rotten planking and putty-filled holes). Her mast and topmast towered higher than those of any vessel ever before seen at Hammersmith; she attracted crowds of admirers from the neighbouring slums. But, alas! it was soon discovered that her beauty was skin deep indeed. Her decks, when an attempt was made to scrape them, came away in lumps of tinder, so that half the planks had to be replaced by new ones. Then her mast was found to be dangerously unsound at the usual spot – where the spar traverses the deck – so a new mast had to be bought. There was no end to the useless and unworkmanlike patching: each day revealed some fresh defect; and though the young man was dismayed at the expense, his friend the boat-maker tinkered cheerfully on, as sanguine as ever in his opinion that the craft would shortly be fit to sail to Spain.

A new stern-post and rudder were found to be necessary; a huge piece of lead was actually put on the rotten and loosened keel; a new suit of sails was ordered for her; no expense was spared in luxuriously fitting out her cabin. At last, on coming down to visit her one morning at high tide, the dismayed owner could see nothing of his beloved vessel save her masts rising above the Thames's turbid stream. She had foundered at her moorings. Bumping on the hard gravel at each low tide, the old craft's bottom had been knocked in; for she could not bear the weight of her own ballast when unsupported by the water. The boat-builder would have gladly undertaken to raise her, repair her bottom, and make her what he was pleased to call 'seaworthy' again. But the young man had had enough of it; he had at last come to his senses. After having thrown away several hundreds of pounds – he might have built an excellent ten-ton cruiser for less – he realised that to patch up a hull so rotten that the bolts, when any strain was put upon them, dragged through the timbers as through so much tinder (they pulled the chain-plates out of her on one occasion when setting up the rigging) was a sheer waste of money, and that he could never hope to sail to Gravesend, far less to Spain, with such a craft. So he wisely abandoned her, and she was rapidly broken up by the wash of penny steamers bumping her crazy frame against the hard foreshore. This experience sickened him of yachting, so he deserted the water, took to the road, and bought himself a buggy, I trust with happier results.

The above may be an extreme instance, and the young man in question was exceptionally green; but I dare say that several readers of this work went through experiences of a somewhat similar description – I know well I did – when they first undertook to purchase cheap old yachts and fit them out for sea. The following are some of the most ordinary precautions that must be observed when selecting a second-hand craft; and if the novice has a friend experienced in nautical matters, he will do well to take him with him when the examination of the vessel on which he has set his affections is to be made.

When surveying an old vessel, thrust a penknife into various portions of her planking and timbers in order to discover whether these be sound or are soft and rotten in places. Do this more especially in the parts most liable to decay – for example, in the planking between wind and water, in all closed and ill-ventilated places, as in the sail-locker, where dry-rot frequently appears. Closely inspect the stern and stern posts. As a rule, the timbers of a yacht can be seen by opening her cabin lockers, but in order to effect a more thorough examination of her frame, remove the ballast in places, and if possible take out some of the cabin panelling. If any repairs are in progress, observe the sawdust brought out by the gimlet; it is powdery if the wood is unsound.

Examine her nails and bolts to see whether she be 'nail-sick,' as the sailors call it – that is, if they have worked loose by the straining of the vessel, or are corroded. Remember that to renail a vessel is an expensive business.

The exterior of the vessel and the keel must be examined when she is high and dry. If she is coppered, her sheathing will reveal whether she has been strained, or has suffered injury by running aground with violence. Horizontal or diagonal wrinkles on the copper show that the vessel has been strained. Vertical wrinkles, unless extending over a large surface, may, as a rule, be disregarded; they merely show that the side has been rubbed against some hard surface. If the horizontal wrinkles are regular, and extend along a great part of the vessel's length, she should be condemned; for these show that her frame has been so loosened by age or severe straining that her shape undergoes a considerable change when she is taken out of the water: she settles down, not being able to support her own weight. The fact that doors and lockers that open and shut readily when she is afloat will not do so when she is high and dry indicates the same condition.

See whether the vessel be copper or iron fastened. Iron fastening is far the least expensive, and is the stronger so long as it lasts; for a copper bolt, being softer, cannot be driven firmly home into hard wood as an iron bolt can. But, on the other hand, iron fastenings are apt to corrode rapidly, and an old iron-fastened vessel is likely to be nail-sick and to require refastening.

It must not be forgotten, too, that copper and iron, when immersed together in sea-water, set up galvanic action; so that if an iron-fastened vessel be coppered, even though the greatest care was taken to prevent contact between the metals when the sheathing was put on, the insidious galvanic action may be at work in places, and the corrosion of the iron nails will be revealed by the presence of iror-rust stains at the junctures of the copper plates. Again, if, as sometimes happens, the sheathing has been brought down into close proximity with the iron keel, the bolts holding the keel may be eaten through, and cases have been known of a vessel's keel falling off when she is under way, in consequence of the unsuspected corrosion of the bolts from this cause. So, too, is it when lead and iron come into contact. Look to the fastenings of the lead keel, if there be one, for if, as is often the case even with copper-fastened vessels, the floor-bolts be of iron, galvanic action may have been set up between the bolts and the lead ballast, and an examination may lead to the timely discovery that the bolt-heads are rotted through, and are ready to fall off.

The great strain of a vessel's rigging comes upon the chain-plates, so the planking and timbers surrounding them should be closely inspected. An old or weakly constructed vessel is often deformed and pulled out of shape by this strain.

Examine the masts and spars to see if they are rotten or sprung. Masts are most liable to be unsound where they pass through the deck, and beneath the hounds. Longitudinal cracks in spars are immaterial unless the fissures be of great depth. It is the custom to fill these cracks with putty in order to keep out the moisture; take out a portion of the putty in places so as to ascertain whether rot has set up within. Transverse or diagonal cracks generally indicate that the spar is sprung, and should be condemned. If the examination of hull and spars proves satisfactory, there yet remains a careful inspection of all the equipment, the condition of the wire and rope rigging, the blocks and sails, the anchor, chain, and so forth.

The age of the vessel must also be taken into consideration before completing the purchase. It is a risky thing to buy an old craft of, say, twenty-five years of age, and at any rate she should be most minutely surveyed. On the other hand a vessel that has been built of honest stuff, and has been well cared for, will remain sound for a great many years; and if, after close examination of an old vessel, she proves to be in really good condition, you may safely trust her more than you would a younger boat. With boats it is as with human beings. Even as a human life is more secure after it has safely passed the period of infantile ailments, so, too, the vessel that has knocked about for years is to be relied on if she still shows no symptoms of decay. Her original constitution must have been sound; her timbers must have been properly seasoned before she was put together; she could not have been scamped and have been built of sappy rubbish. When sappy timber has been employed, dry-rot invariably breaks out within a few years.

A good stout old vessel, for example, was my yawl, the *Alerte*, of fifty-six tons, yacht measurement. She was nearly thirty years old when I crossed the North and South Atlantic in her, and lay hove-to for months in the often stormy sea off the desert island of Trinidade, while my companions were on shore searching for the hidden treasure which was never found. She was built by Ratsey of Cowes in 1864, of honest teak, in days when loving care was taken in the building of a boat, and scamping was not so rife as now. Her every plank had been carefully selected, and had been lying seasoning for years in the builder's loft, ere used. When I bought her she was as sound throughout as when she first came off the stocks; in not a single spot was decay visible.

2

The Effect of the Wind on a Boat

When a boat is floating on the water with sail set, the wind, as will be explained in this chapter, produces on her various effects. It tends to heel her over; to propel her forward; to drive her sideways away from the wind; and to turn one end or other of her round, according to the balance of her sails and the distribution of her weight.

By a scientific construction of hull, sails, and rudder, these different effects are so utilised or counteracted as to enable the helmsman to sail his vessel in any direction he pleases, and even to work the apparent miracle of making her travel against wind and tide combined, with the aid of his canvas only. Those who wish to master the whole theory of sailing, and the scientific adaptation of a vessel to the forces of wind and water, must be referred to larger works than this. The principles that govern the arts of sailing and boat-building carefully and clearly set forth in Mr Dixon Kemp's books. It is the author's intention in this chapter to confine himself to the elements of a subject concerning which every would-be sailor should know something; for in the art of sailing, as in every other art, the novice who takes the trouble to understand a little of the theory, will all the quicker acquire the practice.

HEELING – STABILITY

One of the above-mentioned effects of the wind on a sailing-boat is to heel her over. This effect, being wholly antagonistic to the object for which a boat is built – her forward progression – has to be resisted by giving her sufficient stability. Most of us remember how the model boats we used to carve out of blocks of deal in our boyhood lacked stability when placed in the water, and, refusing to float upright, swam on their sides until we had placed lead on their keels. If a boat is long and narrow, it is as impossible for her to maintain an upright position in the water as for a plank to float on its edge, for in that position her centre of gravity is high above the water-line; she is, in short, top-heavy, and must fall over till she assumes a position in which she is in stable equilibrium.

To give her stability, therefore, her centre of gravity must be lowered. This is done by placing ballast in her bottom, or by putting lead or iron on her keel; and it is obvious that the lower the weight the more effective it will be. A deep boat with a heavy lead keel cannot capsize. She heels over readily to the wind at first, but becomes stiffer as the angle increases; for the more she heels over to the wind, with the greater leverage does her lead keel tend to right her again, and the greater force must the wind exert in order to heel her further. A Lake Windermere yacht, for example, can heel over till she lies flat on her beam ends, and yet rights herself briskly the moment the pressure of the squall diminishes.

On the other hand, a broad, shallow boat needs no ballast to enable her to float upright. Thus the ordinary, beamy, flat-floored, cat-boat of America, with its wooden centre-board, is as often as not sailed without ballast. Such a boat is very stiff at first; she does not heel readily; but having no heavy keel to right her, she capsizes so soon as she has heeled beyond a certain angle.

Of the effects of the wind on a vessel, the one which has to be utilised to the utmost extent is the propelling effect; therefore every boat is constructed so that the water may offer the least resistance to her forward motion. Thus the bow is made sharp, like a wedge, so that it cuts through the water easily and with little friction; while the stern is tapered off gently – the boat, if she be properly built, having what is termed a clean run, which enables the water to glide away from her stern without fuss, instead of forming a following wave to act as a drag on her speed, as is the case if the stern be finished off too abruptly.

LATERAL RESISTANCE – LEEWAY

But when a boat is sailing with the wind on her side, the effect of the wind is not only to drive her forwards, but sideways as well, and she makes what is called leeway. A boat of very shallow draft will, when close-hauled, drift bodily to leeward, and make no headway at all. This tendency to make leeway has to be checked as much as possible by increasing the lateral resistance of the water; and this done by giving the boat a deep keel or a centre-board, or by otherwise providing an extensive area of lateral surface below the water-line.

The lateral resistance opposed by the water to a ship's side acts through a point which is, roughly speaking, the centre of the immersed portion of the vessel's side, and this point is termed the *Centre of Lateral Resistance*. Thus, in Fig. 1 (p.111), *a* is the centre of lateral resistance. A rope made fast to the vessel's side at this point would tow her broadside on; but were it made fast before or aft of that point, the resistance would be greater on one side than on the other, and the rope would pull either the stern or the bow round, as the case might be.

It will be explained further on how the centre of lateral resistance has to be taken into account when the arrangement of the sail-plan is being determined.

ACTION OF THE WIND WHEN THE VESSEL IS CLOSE-HAULED

It is easy to understand how a sailing-boat can travel before a favourable wind, but it would at first sight seem contrary to the laws of dynamics that a boat should be able to sail close-hauled – that is, in a direction opposed to the wind, which serves as the propelling force. A boat, with a sufficiently deep keel to check the tendency to make leeway, can sail within 45 degrees of the wind. In Fig. 2 (p. 111) is represented the deck-plan of a boat sailing close-hauled. The direction of the wind is shown by the arrow W. AB is the sail, so trimmed as just to hold the wind without shaking. Now it can be mathematically demonstrated that the wind, so far as it affects the motion of the vessel, exerts a horizontal pressure on the sail, acting in a direction at right angles to the plane of the sail – that is, in the direction AC. This force, it will be observed, while pressing the boat sideways, tends also to a lesser extent to propel her in a forward direction. The old friend of our youthful studies, the parallelogram of forces, enables us to resolve the force AC into its two component forces, and to estimate their relative magnitudes. Let GF be the line of the keel. From C draw CD perpendicular to GF, and complete the parallelogram ADCE. Then if DC represents the magnitude of the force driving the vessel sideways, AD will represent the magnitude of the force propelling her forward in the direction FG. The closer to the wind a vessel sails, the greater will be the disproportion between these two forces; and the tyro will soon discover that if he flattens his sheets too close and attempts to squeeze his craft too near the wind, so small a proportion of the wind's force will be exerted in propelling his vessel in a forward direction that she will practically stand still. A comparison of Figs. 2 and 3 (p. 111) will demonstrate this. In Fig. 2 the boat is sailing as near the wind as she can, so that the force DC is far greater than the force AD, and she will have little headway. In Fig. 3 the boat is sailing with the wind a little before the beam, so that the propelling force AD is about equal to DC, and she will be travelling fast. As has already been explained, a boat is so constructed as to offer the least possible resistance to the propelling force AD, and, on the other hand – by giving her as large an immersed horizontal section as possible – to offer the utmost resistance to the lateral force DC.

TACKING

It has been explained that a properly constructed boat can sail within 45 degrees of the wind. If the wind be right ahead, or nearly so, what is known as tacking must be resorted to; that is, the boat is made to sail for a certain distance close-hauled with the wind on one side, and is then made to turn and sail close-hauled with the wind on the other side. When sailing V with the wind on her right side, she is said to be on the starboard tack; with the wind on the left side she is on the port tack. In Fig. 4

(p. 114) a boat is tacking right in the teeth of the wind, represented by the arrow W. She sails the same distance on each tack, each tack being at about right angles to the last. In Fig. 5 (p. 112) the wind is not right ahead, but a little on one side of the vessel's course. To attain the desired point, she is therefore made to sail further on one tack than she does on the other, making what the sailors call a long and a short leg.

CENTRE OF EFFORT

Of the various effects of the wind upon the sails of a vessel, the last we have to deal with is its tendency to blow either the vessel's bow or stern round if the sails are not properly balanced. If, for example, a boat sailing with the wind abeam carry too much sail forward – and more especially if the leverage of the head sail, as is the case with a jib, be increased by setting it at the end of a long bowsprit – the boat's bow will be driven off the wind, and the steersman will have to counteract this tendency with the rudder.

Now, the wind exerting a side pressure on a boat's sail, or sails, acts through a point known as the *centre of effort* of the sails – a point which is, roughly speaking, in the centre of the total sail area. It has already been explained that the resistance of the water to a vessel's leeway acts through a point in the centre of the submerged section of the ship's side, known as the centre of lateral resistance. These two horizontal forces act in opposite directions; consequently, unless as in Fig. 6 (p. 113), A, the centre of effort of the sails, and B, the centre of lateral resistance, are in the same vertical line, so that the opposing forces balance each other, the vessel will have a tendency to turn either her bow or her stern towards the wind.

In Fig. 7 (p. 113) we have a vessel sailing close-hauled. Here B, the centre of lateral resistance, is further aft than the centre of effort A. Now, it is obvious that two forces acting at A and B, in the direction of the arrows, will tend to turn the vessel's bow round in the direction of C – that is, away from the wind.

In Fig. 8 (p. 113), on the other hand, the centre of lateral resistance is further forward than the centre of effort; consequently the vessel's bow will have a tendency to turn towards the wind in the direction D.

When a vessel's bow shows a tendency to run up into the wind, she is said to carry *weather helm*; when she shows a tendency to fall off before the wind, she is said to carry *lee helm*. A sailing-boat should always carry a little weather helm; then, if a squall strike her when she has little steerageway and the rudder is useless, she will take care of herself, luff quickly up into the wind, and so be in safety. A boat carrying lee helm would, in the same conditions, fall off before the wind, presenting her broadside to wind and wave, and so probably capsize.

The novice, who has carefully read this chapter, will understand what principles should guide him when he sets to work to correct whichever of the two faults his craft may display – lee helm or excessive weather helm – for the latter makes it necessary to keep the rudder over to leeward at a sharp angle, thus offering great resistance to the water and checking the boat's speed.

A boat carries weather helm when the centre of lateral resistance is further forward than the centre of effort of the sails.

A boat carries lee helm when the centre of lateral resistance is further aft than the centre of effort of the sails.

Thus to reduce weather helm we can either move the centre of lateral resistance further aft or the centre of effort of the sails further forward. By shifting the ballast so as to lighten the vessel forward, and make her heavier aft, we increase the submerged area of her after section, and so move back the centre of lateral resistance. By shortening her after canvas, as by taking in her mizzen, or by increasing her head canvas, as by setting a larger jib, the centre of the effort of the sails is moved forward.

Again, if it be found that a boat carry lee helm under canvas, it shows that either her ballast must be shifted forward, or that the area of her head canvas must be reduced.

ACTION OF THE RUDDER

The action of the rudder is not difficult to understand. By its aid the sailor can steer his vessel in the required direction, and if she carry – as she should do – slight weather helm, he counteracts this, and keeps her on her course, by putting his tiller a little over to the weather side of the boat, and so pushing the rudder over to the lee side.

A reference to Fig. 9 (p. 114) will make clear the action of the rudder. Here the rudder has been pushed over to the port, or left, side of the vessel. The resistance of the water flowing by it acts in the direction of the arrow, at right angles to the rudder's surface. This force is resolvable into two other forces, one pushing the boat backwards, and the other driving the boat's stern sideways to starboard – that is, to the right, and consequently turning the bow to port. But the axis on which the boat turns when the rudder is placed at an angle with the keel is always considerably forward of the centre of the boat, so that the stern of the boat is moved sideways a greater distance than the bow. This will be apparent on referring to Fig. 9, in which X is the centre of rotation, while the dotted line shows the movement the boat has made in response to her tiller. It is important to remember this fact when steering close to a boat or other object; for when one puts over the helm in order to keep one's bow clear of the object, one is very apt by that very action to bring one's stern into collision with it.

Some boats do not readily obey their rudders, are slow in turning, and describe the segment of a large circle in doing so. A boat with its ballast stowed amidships will answer her helm more quickly than one in which the ballast is distributed throughout her length. A boat that draws little water at either extremity, and in which the lateral resistance of the water is concentrated on a deeply immersed midship section, will answer her helm more quickly than a boat whose area of immersed surface is more evenly distributed along the boat's length.

3

Splices, Knots & Tackles

To be familiar with the knots, bends, splices, purchases, in common use at sea is an indispensable qualification for the man who would command his own little vessel; for not only must he know how to handle the various ropes connected with his rigging, belay his sheets and halyards in orthodox fashion, tie his reef-points with the proper knot, and so forth, but he should also be able to effect all ordinary repairs on his rigging – to put a long splice in a broken halyard, for example, or to re-strop a block. This chapter by no means deals fully with this branch of our subject, but it should enable the amateur sailor to acquire a knowledge of the ropes sufficient for all practical purposes.

The cordage employed on a small craft is what is known as hawser-laid. If a hawser-laid or right-hand rope (as it is also called) is opened out, it will be found to consist of three *strands*, each strand being formed of several *yarns*, or threads of hemp twisted together. It is laid 'with the sun' – that is, the strands are twisted together from right to left, the sun's apparent course to one facing north. A hawser-laid rope should be coiled from right to left, with the sun; for if coiled in the reverse direction it will kink, and cannot be made to form a neat and snug coil.

A cable-laid rope is made of three hawser-laid ropes twisted together from left to right, against the sun, and it must be coiled from left to right. The eyes of the rigging, the forestay, and other parts of rigging liable to be chafed, should be wormed, parcelled, and served (see Fig. 10, p. 114).

To worm is to lay spun-yarn in the groove between the strands of a rope, so that a smooth surface is obtained on which the parcelling can be evenly laid. To parcel is to wind narrow strips of well-tarred canvas round the wormed rope, following the lay of the rope, that is, the spiral formed by the strands. Serving a rope consists of winding spun-yarn round the rope, over the parcelling; it is laid against the lay of the rope. While it is being wormed, parcelled, and served, the rope should be stretched out as taut as possible, one end being made fast to the bits or other convenient place, while the other end is hauled out with a tackle. If the rope is a large one, the serving is laid on with a serving mallet.

The free ends of all ropes should be whipped (Fig. 11, p. 114) so as to prevent their unravelling. To do this lay one end of a piece of tarred spun-yarn along the end of the rope; wind the spun-yarn (working upwards towards the end of the rope) several times tightly round the rope and over the end of the spun-yarn, thus gripping the latter. Make a loop of the remaining portion of the spun-yarn, and lay the end of this loop on the rope, pointing downwards away from the rope's end. Then take three or four more turns with the spun-yarn round the rope and over the loose end of the yarn. Pull the yarn-end taut until the loop is closed, and cut the ends short off.

In the following description of the splices, knots, etc., certain terms will be employed which it will be well to define beforehand. The standing part of a rope is the part held in the hand; the end is that end of the rope in which the knot, or bend, is to be made; the bight is the loop formed when making a knot, or bend.

When two rope-ends have to be joined permanently, this is neatly effected by the various splices employed by sailors.

A short splice (Fig. 12, p. 115) is thus made: The two rope-ends that have to be joined are unlaid for a few inches, so that the three strands of which each rope is formed are separated. Each strand-end is greased and twisted up into a point so that it can be easily manipulated. Then the three strands of one rope are so placed across the three strands of the other rope that each strand lies closely between two strands of the rope opposite. Each strand is then passed under the next strand but one to it, of the opposite rope, and is drawn tightly through. The process is repeated, and as a rule each strand is, in all, drawn three times through the alternate strands; but before being passed through for the last time it is tapered, so as to give the splice a neater appearance, by cutting off half the yarns composing it. Lastly, the loose ends are cut off and the spliced part of the rope is hammered into shape with a mallet. In order to open the strands out so as to make way for the ends to pass through, a marlinespike or pricker – which should be well greased – is employed.

When two ropes are connected by a short splice, the spliced part is thicker than the rope itself. But if the ropes are joined by a long splice, the spliced portion is no thicker than the rope, and cantherefore be rove through any block which will take the rope. Consequently the long splice must always be used for repairing a halyard, sheet, or other part of the rigging which has to run through blocks.

A long splice is thus made: the two ropes that are to be joined are unlaid for at least four times as far as would be the case if making a short splice. The strands are brought together as in the short splice; then one strand of each rope (*a, a,* in Fig. 13, p. 115) is unlaid for a still further distance (about half as far again). This leaves two grooves in the rope, which are next filled up by neatly laying in each of them the opposite central strands *b, b.* This brings the strands together in pairs in three places as in Fig. 14 (p. 115). At these three points the strands are reduced in thickness by cutting off half the yarns, as when completing a shortsplice. Each pair of strands is tied in an overhand knot, and the ends are tucked under the alternate strands opposite as in a short splice. The rope is, lastly, well stretched with tackle, and the projecting ends of the divided strands are cut off.

When a rope's end has to be spliced round a block or thimble, an eye-splice (Fig. 15, p. 116) is employed. To make this, the end of the rope is unlaid and the strands are spliced into the standing part of the rope in the same way as when making a short splice.

A cut splice (Fig. 16, p. 116) is formed with two ropes by splicing the end of each into the standing part of the other as in an eye-splice. On a small yacht the shrouds are sometimes fitted over the hounds with a cut-splice, and this is neater than having two shrouds with a separate eye in each.

If one strand of a rope be cut through, the damage can be made good by removing a long piece of the injured strand and by laying in the groove thus left a new strand from another piece of similar rope. The ends are then knotted, halved, and turned under, as when making a long splice.

A grommet, a useful rope-ring, is thus made: a strand is removed from a rope, care being taken to preserve its spiral score, which serves as a guide in the construction of the grommet. One end of the strand is bent round and laid on the standing part so as to form a ring of the required size. Then the other end is wound round this ring twice, fitting into the score, and so forming a three-stranded rope. The ends are knotted, halved, and turned under as in a long splice.

The following are the more useful knots, bends, and hitches employed at sea for temporarily attaching ropes. They are all ingeniously contrived so as to hold securely and not to slip, while they can yet be undone easily and quickly, and do not jam like some of the wonderful and inextricable knots the greenhorn is apt to tie when carrying out an order in a hurry.

The overhand knot (Fig. 17, p. 117) is the knot which, as has already been stated, is tied in the strands when completing a long splice or a grommet.

Fig. 18 (p. 117) is a reef knot. The reef-points of a sail are tied up with this knot, and it is also frequently of service for other purposes. It consists of two overhand knots. In tying the second knot care must be taken so to cross the ends that the standing part and end of each rope pass through the bight of the other rope together, and not from opposite sides, as they do in the *Granny*, of which a diagram is given (Fig. 19, p. 117), so as to show the novice what he must studiously avoid making if he would avoid much chaff from the older hands.

The common bend (Fig. 20, p. 117) is useful for bending two ropes together. A bight is made with the end of one rope. The end of the other rope is passed through the bight, round both parts of the bight, and under its own standing part. The bend is then pulled taut.

Two half hitches (Fig. 21, p. 118) are used for bending a rope to a spar, a boat's painter to a dolphin, or a mooring-ring on the quay, etc.

A clove hitch (Fig. 22, p. 118) is used to make fast a small rope to a larger standing rope or to a spar. Thus the ratlines are tied to the N shrouds with clove hitches. When a rope has to be (Fig. 22) bent on a spar quickly, this can be done by means of a timber hitch (Fig. 23, p. 119). When jammed tight it will not slip; yet it can be cast off in a moment.

When a rope has to be attached temporarily to a hook *(e.g.* to the hook of a tackle) in order to get a pull on it, a black wall hitch (Fig. 24, p. 119) is employed.

When a rope has to be made fast to another rope in order to haul upon it, a rolling hitch (Fig. 25, p. 120) is used, as this will not slip down if properly made. Thus, when a shroud has to be hauled out taut for setting up, the tail end of the tackle is fastened to the shroud with this hitch. In the figure the hitch appears with its parts loose; but these, of course, have to be drawn together and jammed before applying the strain.

To form a loop in a rope that will not slip or jam, a bowline knot is employed. To make this knot (Fig. 26, p. 160) a little practice is required.

In a running bowline (Fig. 27, p. 120) the loop made by the bowline knot runs, standing part of the rope, thus forming a sheepshank.

A bowline on a bight (Fig. 28, p. 121) is a bowline made after a different fashion on the doubled rope. It is used when the knot has to be made in the middle of the rope at a distance from the ends.

With a fisherman's bend (Fig. 29, p. 121) a rope can be very securely fastened to an anchor shackle, or mooring-ring. When employed for bending one's cable on to the anchor, the end of the rope should be seized on the standing part, as in the figure, with a piece of stout twine.

Gaff topsail halyards are generally bent on the topsail yard with a topsail halyard bend, which cannot slip if properly made and drawn close.

This bend (Fig. 30, p. 121) is made by taking three turns round the yard with the halyard, leading it back over the standing part, under the three turns, and back under the first turn.

The topsail sheet is bent to the cringle of the topsail with a topsail sheet bend (Fig. 31, p. 122).

A Sheepshank (Fig. 32, p. 122) is employed to shorten a rope ternporarily, e.g. a topmast shroud, when the topmast is lowered. On most yachts, however, nowadays, wire topmast shrouds are used instead of hemp ones, each shroud having two joints, so that when the topmast is housed, the lowest joint is unshackled and stowed away, and the upper joint, being just of the right length, is set up with the tackle or lanyards.

There are various tackle and purchases employed on a yacht's rigging, by which mechanical advantage is gained; but of course what is gained in power is lost in time. Thus a system of pulleys that enables a pull of five pounds to raise fifty pounds, involves the hauling of ten times the length of rope through the blocks than would be the case were no purchase used. On a small yacht, therefore, where it is important that sails should be hoisted and lowered quickly, no purchase should be more powerful than is absolutely necessary, that is, it should just enable one man to do the particular work for which it is employed. To overblock a little yacht entails a delay in every operation, and an increased risk of ropes jamming.

The following are the tackles and purchases in common use on small yachts:

The single-whip purchase (Fig. 33, p. 122) has a single block. This is the purchase employed for the fore and jib halyards of a small cutter; the block, as is explained in the chapter on a cutter's rigging, being hooked on to the cringle of the sail. A pull of one pound on the hauling part puts a strain of two pounds on the block.

The whip-upon-whip purchase (Fig. 34, p. 122) is employed for the preventer backstays on small cutters. A pull of one pound on the hauling part exerts a force of four pounds at the upper block.

The gun-tackle purchase (Fig. 35, p. 122) has two single blocks with the standing part of the rope made fast to the upper block. A pull of one pound on the hauling part exerts a force of three pounds at the upper block. This purchase can be employed for bowsprit shrouds, main tack tricing line, etc.

A luff-tackle purchase (Fig. 36, p. 122) has the same power as the whip-upon-whip purchase. It has one single and one double block, the standing part of the tackle being fastened to the single block. It is used for a variety of purposes, among others for the main sheet on a small cutter.

A watch tackle is a luff tackle with a tail – a rope some feet in length – on the double block, and a hook on the single block. A watch tackle should always be kept in some convenient place on a yacht's deck, for it is employed on all sorts of odd jobs when more 'beef' is wanted. It is indeed almost worth an extra hand on board, so sailors dub it the 'Handy Billy'. Among other things it is useful for setting up the rigging. It is employed as follows: the single block is hooked on to a ring-bolt on deck, or to a strop or bight of a rope secured to the bits or other strong piece of timber; while the tail of the double block is fastened by a rolling hitch (see Fig. 25, p. 120) to the shroud or rope which has to be hauled taut.

Power can be multiplied when necessary, by clapping one purchase on another. A luff-upon-luff tackle, for example, is formed with two watch tackles by bending the tail of the double block of the second tackle on the fall of the first tackle. A pull of one pound on the hauling part will then exert a force of sixteen pounds at the further end of the tackle.

If some accident happen to one part of a tackle or purchase – if a strand be chafed through, for example – and it becomes necessary to repair the damage, while at the same time it is undesirable to slack up the tackle, or to take it from the work it is doing (e.g. in the case of a yacht's halyards or sheets during a close race), the tackle can be racked while the repair is being carried on. Thus, if the hauling part of the throat halyards be cut, the other three or more parts of the halyards are racked by passing a piece of thin line round and between them several times tightly, and then tying the two ends of the line together with a reef knot. This grips the parts, prevents the halyard from running through the blocks, and enables them to hold on and withstand the strain put upon them, while the injured part is cast loose and repaired at leisure.

Some of the blocks used on board a yacht – those, for example, which are hooked on to the mast for the throat and peak halyards – are usually stropped with iron; and in the neatly finished blocks, the iron is covered by the shell of the block. But for other parts of the rigging ordinary blocks are employed; and the amateur sailor should know how to splice an eye in the end of a piece of hemp or wire rope for the strop of a tail block, and how to make a grommet, or a selvagee strop.

I have already explained how to splice an eye in a rope, and how to make a grommet. For stropping a block a selvagee strop is to be preferred to a grommet, though both are used for this purpose. A selvagee strop is thus made: two large nails are firmly driven into a piece of board at a distance apart of about half the circumference of the required strop. One end of a ball of rope-yarn is fastened to one of the nails, and the yarn is wound round the two nails (see Fig. 37, p. 123) as tightly as possible, until the ring thus formed is sufficiently stout. Then the yarns are tied together, or marled, at short intervals, with twine, and lastly the strop is well stretched with tackle.

Grommets made of wire rope can be advantageously employed on a small vessel for the strops of the main-sheet blocks, as such grommets cannot stretch so much as to allow the blocks to slip through them – a not infrequent accident, and a very awkward one, when a rope strop is used.

All strops, whether of rope or wire, whether selvagee strops, grommets, or eye-splices, should be coated with canvas, or, better still, with leather. If coated with canvas, the strop should be painted; if leather is employed, it should be sewn on the strop wet, as it will shrink when dry, and so fit tightly to the strop.

It is well to have a swivel or revolving hook on one of the blocks of any movable tackle forming part of the rigging, for example, on the tackle of the runners and of the preventer backstays. This will enable turns to be taken out of the tackle without unhooking it.

Galvanised clip-hooks (Fig. 38, p. 138) should be spliced into the ends of such parts of rigging as have frequently to be hooked and unhooked. When hooking a clip-hook to an eye, the two parts of the clip-hook are opened out; they are then closed over the eye, one part overlapping the other. The two parts should always be seized together, else they may shake open and release the eye. Mousing is the sailor's name for this operation.

In Fig. 38 is shown the method usually employed on small boats for hooking the jib-sheets on to the clew of the jib by means of clip-hooks. The sheets are formed by one rope, in the middle of which the eye of the clip-hooks is seized with strong twine. Clip-hooks are more convenient than the wooden toggles often used for jib-sheets, and are also to be preferred to spring clip-hooks, which are apt to shake open despite the spring which is supposed to keep them closed.

4

The Small Open Sailing Boat

A small boat that can be sailed single-handed without difficulty, and which is easy to row – so that, if the wind fails, one can put out the sculls and pull her along at a fair pace – is the best sort of craft on which the novice can pass his early apprenticeship. That he can lower his canvas if he finds himself in a difficulty, and take to his oars, considerably lessens the risk consequent on his inexperience.

This chapter will be confined to the description of *open* boats only, of various sorts; for a boat so small that she can be easily rowed should not be covered in, nor be half-decked. A half-decked boat – that is, one decked in the bows and stern, and having a narrow deck with coamings on either side – is in some respects safer than an open boat; if struck by a squall she can heel over to a much greater angle without shipping water than would be possible were she open. But when a small boat is thus half-decked, her owner is apt to imagine that he is in possession, not of a boat, but of a small yacht, and is likely to over-spar her, overballast her, and over-canvas her, consequently to over-sail her. She will no longer be the sort of boat I am now recommending – one easy to sail and easy to row. The decking occupies more room than can well be spared in a small boat, and one is cramped on board. The decking is also weighty, and tends to make the boat top heavy, so that to counteract this she requires more ballast and becomes a heavy boat, difficult to beach, hard to pull, wet in a seaway. On many parts of the coast fishermen have a strong objection to decking even the bows of their small craft, and maintain that the deck offers great resistance to the wind, so that the vessel is pressed down, and is not nearly so buoyant as if she were open. It is certain that, other things being equal, the open boat is the liveliest and the best sea boat. The half-decked boat is only to be recommended when the craft is big enough to be practically a small yacht, with a cuddy under the decking forward. The above remarks, of course, do not apply to boats intended for racing. These, however small, must, as a rule, be heavily ballasted, and may be partly decked.

The following observations apply to small sailing and rowing boats of all classes:

CLINKER AND CARVEL BUILT BOATS

Small boats are generally clinker-built. In a clinker-built boat the planks overlap each other, whereas a carvel-built boat presents a smooth surface. The clinker-built boat has very light framework to support the planking. The carvel-built boat is put together much in the same way as a big vessel – that is, she has a framework of solid timbers to which the planking is fastened.

The carvel-built boat has the following advantages over the clinker-built boat: she is much stronger, will last longer, and is more easily repaired; thus, if a portion of her planking has been damaged, it can be easily replaced, whereas, it is difficult to patch the planking of a clinker-built boat. When the carvel-built craft lies at anchor, the tide ripples almost silently along her smooth sides, whereas against the irregular surface of the clinker-built boat the water ever splashes noisily, and at night is apt to disturb the slumbers of one unaccustomed to roughing it on a small boat.

On the other hand, the clinker-built boat is much cheaper than the carvel-built; she is lighter – an important consideration when a boat is intended for rowing and for hauling up on a beach. The clinker-built boat is also more buoyant and lively in a seaway; for the edges of the overlapping planks extending horizontally and facing downwards offer considerable resistance to the water, so that the boat is lifted by every wave. When everything is taken into consideration, there can be little doubt that for the class of boats with which I am dealing in this chapter the clinker-build is to be preferred.

CONSTRUCTION OF THE BOAT

Remember, when selecting your craft, that a boat constructed of pine or Swedish fir is not only the cheapest, but is also the lightest, and, *ceteris paribus,* should out-sail and out-row a boat built of heavier material; but, on the other hand, she will not last long, and the soft wood readily gets torn and bruised. The top streak of a fir-built boat should be of cedar, or of some hard wood.

If the boat is to be frequently beached or subjected to other rough treatment, it is better that she should be built of elm or oak.

BALLASTING

The ballast of a small boat, more especially if she has to be frequently drawn up on a beach, should be so arranged that it can be readily removed. Iron or lead blocks, of half a hundredweight each, with handles to them, are a very convenient form of ballast for a small boat; for they can be easily lifted out. Battens should be fastened to the floor of the boat to keep the ballast in its place; as otherwise, when the boat has listed in a squall, the ballast might fall to leeward, and so cause a capsize. As metal ballast is heavier than any other, it can be stowed low, more especially if it is moulded to fit into the flooring; and consequently the boat ballasted with it will be stiffer under canvas, and will sail faster than one ballasted with a more bulky material, such as stones or sand.

The risks of sailing are much reduced for the novice if his craft is unsinkable. If a boat will float though full of water, her owner, in the event of a capsize, can hold on to her side until some one comes to his rescue; and in most cases his craft also will be recovered undamaged, whereas a boat of higher specific gravity, sinking in deep water, will in all probability be lost. Water, therefore, though somewhat bulky, is the safest form of ballast that can be used, and is strongly recommended to the tyro. Iron or zinc water-tanks should be constructed to fit closely into the bottom of the boat amidships. A boat thus ballasted is practically no heavier when filled with water after a capsize than if she had no ballast at all in her; for the weight of the tanks themselves is inconsiderable. By means of a small pump, the tanks can be readily filled or emptied at will – a great advantage; for, by discharging the water ballast, one can materially lighten the boat when one lowers the sail to take to the oars, or when one is about to run her on the beach and haul her up. If lead or iron ballast be employed, the boat should be made unsinkable by placing in her water-tight compartments, which thus convert her into a lifeboat. One compartment in the bows, and another in the stern-sheets will suffice, and, if made to fit closely, they occupy but little room.

Bags of sand are sometimes used for ballasting small boats; but these are clumsy to handle, occupy a lot of room, and greatly increase in weight when the sand gets wet.

I have already explained in Chapter 2 that the leeway of a boat, or her tendency to drift sideways when she is sailing with the wind before the beam, must be counteracted by giving her a deep keel, or by otherwise providing an area of lateral surface below the water-line, and thus increasing the lateral resistance.

One of the author's first sailing-craft was an old ship's boat, recovered from a vessel that was wrecked at the mouth of the Seine, to which he affixed a false keel in order to prevent leeway. The false keel (of wood) was bolted on to the original keel, and attained its greatest depth, of about six inches, a little abaft the middle of the boat, tapering up towards the bow and stern. This is an inexpensive method of converting an old open boat into a fairly good sailing-craft. A centre-board, however – which I shall shortly describe – is far more effective as a preventer of leeway; for with a given area of immersed lateral surface, the keel that is deep but not long (like the centre-board) offers the greatest lateral resistance to the water. A centre-board boat is also handier and quicker in stays than an open boat provided with a false keel.

The boat provided with a false keel is unsuitable for an open coast where beaching is frequently necessary, or for shallow water. If these be the conditions of sailing, the boat should have a shallow keel and a flat floor. A sharp boat ploughs through the sand or shingle on being hauled up, whereas the flat-floored boat is drawn up with little labour, and is not so likely to strain herself when taking the ground in a surf. The beach boat should be provided with bilge pieces (Fig. 39, p. 124). These keels, running along a great portion of the bilge on either side, should be of hard wood, and be so placed that they take all the wear and tear when the boat is being beached; without them a boat's planking is soon knocked to pieces by beaching. Bilge keels increase the lateral resistance, and so to some extent lessen leeway; but unless they be so large as to be clumsy and to interfere considerably with the boat's speed, they are, so far as the author's experience goes, generally insufficient by themselves to enable a boat to beat to windward in a satisfactory manner; and a centre-board or lee-boards will be found necessary.

THE COBLE

There is, however, one sort of boat (one hesitates to recommend it to the novice, for it is a tricky and somewhat difficult craft to handle) which, while admirably adapted for beaching, yet sails very well indeed to windward, even through a heavy sea, without the aid of centre-board or lee-board. This is the coble of Northumberland, possibly the best open boat in the world for a harbourless stormy coast. The coble is easy to row, safe to beach, and can be launched and put to sea even in very rough weather. The coble (Fig. 40, p. 124) has a considerable draught of water forward; her keel, deepest at the bows, tapers away to nothing amidships, so that abaft that point she has a perfectly flat floor, and draws very little water. This deep bow and the rudder, which is large and descends far below the boat's bottom, provide sufficient lateral resistance to stop the leeway. It will be noticed that the bow is high and flaring, so that the coble rises to the seas, and is not readily swamped.

When a coble is to be beached, the rudder is unshipped, the stern is turned to the shore, and she is backed in with the oars until her flat stern grounds. Both when launching and beaching her high bow is thus presented to the surf; it is astonishing to see with what safety these boats, skilfully handled, can be carried across the line of the North Sea breakers when the winter wind blows hard on shore.

THE CENTRE-BOARD

The most effective method of preventing the leeway of a small boat is to provide her with a centre-board. The centre-board, now so familiar to all who boat on English waters, is generally constructed of iron, but if lightness is an important consideration, it might be better to have it of wood, as is often the case with the American boats. On the other hand, the iron centre-board acts as ballast, and, being so deeply immersed, produces a far greater effect in stiffening the boat than would a much greater weight of iron stowed inside of her. The centre-board is generally of triangular shape. When hauled up it is contained in a water-tight trunk, or case, in the body of the boat; it works on a pivot at its fore end, and when lowered passes through the centre of the keel. When the boat strikes on a shoal, the centre-board is forced up into the trunk, and warns the steersman that it is time to go about or make for deeper water. If the centre-board is not jammed, it rarely bends or breaks when the boat runs on shore; but this does occasionally occur. It is better to employ an iron handle than a chain for hauling up the centre-board. The handle has a joint, so that it can be doubled back and be laid snugly along the top of the trunk when the centre-board is up. The advantage of the handle is that by forcing it down one can release the centre-board if the latter be jammed, as not unfrequently happens, by pebbles or bits of wood or weed that have found their way into the trunk.

The centre-board trunk occupies a good deal of space in the boat, and is often found to be much in the way. To obviate this, a folding centre-board has been invented which requires no trunk, and which the author has found to answer very well on canoes he has used on American waters. This centre-board consists of three or more plates of iron, at one end working on a pivot in the keel, and made so as to open out and close like a fan. The plates are hauled up or lowered by a rod working in a tube which passes through the keel into the boat. When hoisted, the plates fold up and lie snugly alongside each other in a chamber cut into the middle of the keel.

LEE-BOARDS
The simplest method of supplying a boat with the means of offering lateral resistance to the water, and so checking leeway, is to fit her with lee-boards. Lee-boards are not often to be seen in England save on Thames barges; but on the shallow Dutch waters, where small-boat sailing is as well understood as it is here, lee-boards are to be found on nearly every yacht. Lee-boards have several advantages over centre-boards; they do not jam, break off, or strain the boat when one runs aground, but always come up at once on touching the bottom. Some shallow waters (the Danish fjords, for example, among which the author once cruised, in a lee-board boat) are in summer overgrown with weeds, through which a centre-board craft could never force her way: the long water growth would wind round the plate and choke the trunk; on the other hand, a lee-board can always be pulled up without difficulty when it gets foul, and be quickly cleared of the weeds.

If expense is a consideration, the novice cannot do better than fit his first little boat with lee-boards. We will suppose that he has purchased a secondhand craft for a few pounds. To fit a centre-board into her would be a costly bit of work, only to be undertaken by a skilled boat-builder. But any boy who has even a very small experience of the use of carpenter's tools can construct a lee-board and fit it to his boat. The author once placed lee-boards on an old P. and O. lifeboat, and sailed with her from Hammersmith to Copenhagen and back, cruising round the Zuider Zee, coasting up the Frisian islands, winding in and out among the many pleasant fjords, straits, and islands of the Baltic. With her varnished teak sides and oaken lee-boards she looked very well, and her sailing powers were as excellent as her appearance. She was double-ended – that is, her stern was pointed like her bow; she was ketch-rigged; and, drawing little over two feet with her lee-boards up, she could put into all sorts of interesting little creeks and rivers closed to bigger craft. Fig. 41 (p. 125) will give some idea of her appearance and of the shape of her lee-boards. Lee-boards for large boats are made in sections held together by stout iron bands, and are hauled up by chains and tackle; but for a small boat, a lee-board made out of a single plank will do very well, and no iron-work is needed.

Almost anything that can float can be made to sail to windward by lowering a plank vertically over the side; for that is practically all a lee-board amounts to – a fact to be borne in mind when one wishes to extemporise a sailing-craft in some out-of-the-way corner of the world where means and appliances are few. Thus some years ago the author, being in Florida, on the coast of the Gulf of Mexico, took it into his head to undertake a cruise down the shallow channels that divide the mainland from the long line of palmetto-covered *keys* or islands that fringe that beautiful coast. He found nothing in the way of a craft available for his purpose, save what the natives were pleased to call a canoe; she was a little punt, a shallow, clumsily built trough, in shape resembling rather one of the trays in which photographers develop their plates than a boat. He made a sail for her, and then out of a pine plank cut a lee-board about three feet long, shaped as in Fig. 42 (p. 125), stout at the head and down the centre, but tapering away to a narrow edge at the foot and sides. Having determined by experiment at what part of the boat's side the lee-board was most effective, he fitted an iron pin (see the Fig.) on either gunwale. A rope was then rove through the head of the lee-board, and knotted so as to prevent it from slipping through. The other end of the rope was made fast to a cleat at the bottom of the boat amidships. The lee-board could thus be easily thrown over from one side to the other, according to the tack on which the boat was sailing; the rope, being always passed over the fore side of either iron pin, kept the lee-board in its place, and prevented it from sliding aft. Another rope, rove through a hole at the lower end of the lee-board, led aft, and served to raise it. The above is the simplest method of fitting lee-boards, and the result will be found to be perfectly satisfactory. In the punt he has described, the author, provided with rod and gun, for game and fish were plentiful, undertook a long cruise among the bayous and channels of the Gulf Coast, camping out each night in pine forests on the mainland or on the sands of desert key, much astonishing the few natives he met; for a lee-board was an unknown mystery to them, and they marvelled to see one of their rough country punts turn to windward so well when provided with this strange invention. The punt drew but three inches of water when her lee-board was up, and skimmed over the water at a wonderful rate. It must be confessed that she was not a good sea-boat: she had very little freeboard, and was easily swamped. In fact, whenever the wind rose and the water became choppy she was in imminent danger of filling. And yet her skipper felt no anxiety, for the peril was not so great as one would gather from the above statement. The water through which he sailed was generally considerably under two feet in depth, often so shallow that foundering was a physical impossibility. When it got very rough he adopted a bold course. He used to lighten his vessel by stepping out of her into the tossing waters, and, walking ahead of her with tow-line over his shoulder, would tow her against wind and sea until calmer weather permitted him to reembark and hoist his canvas. The working of lee-boards is very simple. When running before the wind they are raised; when turning to windward the weather one is raised and the lee one is lowered.

If a boat's sides are not straight up and down, but flare out, as is usually the case, a chock of wood must be nailed on either side a little above the water-line to support the lee-boards and keep them perpendicular.

The Florida canoe above mentioned was practically what we should call in England a sailing-punt. Such a boat is only suited for sailing in smooth water, and though not exactly beautiful to look upon, she will sail fairly well, and is incontestably the cheapest of all boats to build. Indeed, so simple is the construction, that, if proper instructions, are given to him, any village carpenter can turn out a craft of this description; and an amateur of small means, possessing some knowledge of the use of tools, can build one for himself out of a few deal planks, and some hard wood for stem, keel, and knees. If the boat has a centre-board (which is far more difficult to construct than lee-boards) this should be of wood, not of iron; and, having plenty of beam, she should need no ballast. With such a boat, which with sail, oars, etc., should not cost more than four pounds, the novice can with advantage pass his first apprenticeship at sailing.

Of course, with such a craft one should not venture into rough water. I was compelled to do so once, and passed through strange experiences, in the course of which I made some discoveries as to the seaworthy qualities (in a novel sense of the term, as I shall have to explain) of this sort of boat. It was during the Spanish-American War, and in my capacity of war correspondent of the *Times*, attached to the Spanish side, I was ordered to go to Havana, which was then being blockaded by the United States squadron. Having made several attempts to get through the blockade, either by running it or legitimately, and having failed to accomplish my purpose in consequence of the difficulties put in my way by the American authorities, I had at last to adopt the one plan left open to me. I bought in Key West the only small boat I could find, a flat-bottomed punt such as I have described, fourteen feet in length. She had somewhat more freeboard than most of her class, but still she was the last sort of boat I should have selected for use in rough water. One night I gave the slip to those who were spying my movements, smuggled my boat on to the deck of a little steamer that was starting for the South, and the next morning I was off the Cuban coast. When we were yet six miles off the land my boat was lowered into the water; the skipper would approach no nearer, fearing to draw the fire of the Spanish batteries. My intention was to pull towards the shore, which was there uninhabited and exposed to a heavy surf, land when I found a convenient place, and then walk in the direction of Havana, and hand myself over to the officer of the first party of Spanish troops I should meet with, avoiding, if possible, on my way any encounter with Cuban insurgents or Spanish guerillas, for the Spanish irregulars were known to have an unpleasant habit of shooting first and challenging afterwards. As bad luck would have it, it had been blowing hard for two days, and a nasty sea was running. I knew it was a perilous adventure, and had it not been that there was no other way of carrying out my mission I should not have thought of making the attempt. But I had no choice, so I leapt into the boat from the pitching and rolling steamer, and pulled off alone towards the distant shore.

The steamer stood by for a while to see that all went well with me. The sea was running parallel to the shore, the fresh trade-wind being here nearly always opposed to the strong current of the Gulf Stream. For some time I got on well; but I found that I had to exert the greatest care and vigilance, keeping the boat dead before each high sea, and edging shorewards in the 'smooths'. When I was about a mile from the steamer, which was still lying to, I entered a succession of steep and dangerous seas. A few had rolled safely by me, when there came one which broke just as I was about to top it; a volume of water rushed over the stern of the boat, filling it and then capsizing it. Clinging to the keel with one hand, I held up an oar with the other as a signal to the steamer, which was still lying to. She immediately began to steam ahead, and I took it for granted that she was making for me; but soon, to my dismay, I realised that she had turned, and was proceeding on her voyage, directly away from me. My signal had been mistaken for an intimation that all was right with me. Thus left alone, with but small chance of receiving any assistance, for there were no boats on that portion of the coast, my first idea was to make an attempt to swim for the shore, but I saw that the distance was too great, and that it was extremely unlikely I should reach the land, even if I escaped the sharks that swarm in these waters. Indeed, I saw several while I was clinging on to the boat. I therefore decided to remain with the boat, and taking advantage of a smooth, I succeeded in righting her, but I found that it would be impossible to bale her out, however smooth the sea; for, empty though she was, only her bow and stern rose above the water, her sides being immersed. After trying some experiments with her, I soon discovered that, though the boat was unfit to carry one through a rough sea, she was, in consequence of her breadth and her flat floor, a much better boat to cling on to when swamped and capsized than a far better sea-boat would have been in the same position. This is what I meant when I spoke of her seaworthy qualities. She was frequently rolled over by the waves, now floating keel upwards and now righting herself; but it was always possible for me to lie upon one side or the other without fatiguing myself to any great extent, though I was, of course, up to my shoulders in water, and the waves were constantly passing over my head. Then, holding on to the stern, I swam behind the boat, endeavouring thus to direct her shorewards, but with no appreciable result; and soon, seeing the fin of a shark not far off, I promptly resumed my former position on the boat, where my body was not so exposed to view. I thus drifted until the evening, when the wind freshened and the sea rose, so that the boat's capsizings became more frequent, and the waves dashed over my head more often than before. I had little hope now, and thought it almost certain that, tired out, I should be washed off the boat before the morning. But I contrived to hold on all night, and found myself at dawn not much exhausted. I was now apparently about three miles from the coast, which was evidently unpopulated. The sea was so much smoother that I found it possible to sit in the bottom of the water-logged boat, and, by paddling first on one side and then on the other with the one oar that remained to me (I had lashed it to the thwarts immediately after my capsize), I endeavoured to direct her towards the shore. But it was hopeless work; after I had been thus toiling for hours, the palm-clad hills and yellow sands appeared as far away as ever. While doing this I contrived to balance the boat pretty well; it was only occasionally that she capsized, threw me out, and had to be once more righted. To get into her again when this occurred was no easy matter; for the sea was still choppy, and the boat was apt to roll over with me again before I could get my balance properly.

But I was now pretty well accustomed to her ways, and was able to do with her what I certainly could not have done with the ordinary, deeper, and better sea-boat. When swamped she certainly displayed a remarkable seaworthiness; that may be the wrong term to apply to this quality of hers, but whatever it was it saved my life. Had she been provided with water-tight compartments in her bow and stern, I could have baled her out and got into her so soon as the sea had sufficiently gone down.

At last, with a violent squall, the wind shifted to N.N.E., thus blowing towards the land, instead of parallel to it as before. Here I saw my chance; my hope revived, and I determined to employ all my remaining strength in a struggle to reach the shore. I sat in the stern, and, paddling hard with the oar, I kept the boat before the wind, which, striking her uplifted bows, gave her some way through the water, and I soon discovered that she was making distinct progress. I paddled steadily on for, I should say, three hours, the boat capsizing and having to be righted every quarter of an hour or so. To cut short this long yarn – which, however, may prove instructive, and provide the reader with some useful wrinkles if he ever gets into a similar predicament – I neared the shore, and saw before me a steep rocky beach on which the surf was breaking furiously – a most dangerous place at which to attempt a landing. But the landing had to be made, so I pushed on. When about forty yards from the shore I got into a succession of steep rollers, and the boat gave her final capsize. Springing clear of her, I swam for the shore. Three times I came in on the crest of a wave, was battered and bruised by the rocks, and then carried out to sea again. But the fourth time I succeeded in clinging tightly to a rock, and, before the next wave was on me, scrambled on to dry land, having passed twenty-four hours In the Gulf Stream, rolling over and over with my swamped boat. My capture by Spanish troops, my imprisonment, and my subsequent adventures before I reached the city of Havana – which was not until seven days later – have nothing to do with yachting or boating, so I will not recount them here.

POINTED STERNS

I have already described my P. and O. lifeboat with which I sailed to the Baltic as having a pointed stern. The double-ended boat is far better adapted for use on rough seas than a boat having a square stern. Hence lifeboats and the small fishing-craft of the Baltic and other stormy seas are thus constructed. A good double-ended boat with plenty of sheer – that is, with her bulwarks forming a bold curve from bow to stern – is strongly to be recommended to the tyro. He will find that such a boat will steer far more easily than the usual square-sterned boat when running before a heavy sea. She is then far safer than a boat of any other form. Presenting a sharp wedge to the following rollers, they glide by her and she rises like a duck to each sea. A boat with a square stern, or, worse still, with a counter – an abomination on a small craft – behaves in a very different manner. The following seas, striking her bluff opposing stern with force, are apt to drive her bows under water. or cause her to broach to – that is, force her round with their impact till she is broadside on to the sea, and is in serious danger of being swamped or rolled over by a wave before she can be paid off before the wind again. The sharp-sterned boat is also obviously far the safest to beach through a heavy surf.

THE RIG

After the novice has selected his open boat, it remains for him to decide how he shall rig her. The following are the more usual methods of rigging small open sailing-boats of the class dealt with in this chapter. The rigs I am about to describe require no booms, and are therefore the safest for the novice. A sail that has no boom – a lug, for example – when the sheet is let go in a squall, blows away before the wind like a flag, and cannot capsize the boat. This is not the case with a sail stretched out on a boom, which always offers some resistance to the wind, even when the sheet is let go. With the boomsail a jibe in a strong wind is a risky proceeding. On the other hand, a boat cannot sail her best without a boom; when running before the wind the sail forms a bag, and does not hold so much wind as it would if its foot were extended on a boom. It is only when the boat is on a wind that the boomless sail can be got to stand flat, and then only if the sheet is led well aft and made fast to a place exactly in the line of the foot of the sail. The dipping lug (Fig. 43, p. 126) is much used by fishermen on their open boats; it is a very safe sail when handled by skilled men, but it has some serious disadvantages, and is not to be recommended to the novice. The sail has no boom, and the tack is made fast in the bows; consequently every time the boat goes about or jibes, the sail has to be lowered, passed over to the other side of the mast, and hoisted again. A lug-sailed boat, therefore, cannot well be sailed single-handed, and even when fully manned is a very inconvenient craft for tacking in narrow waters. Moreover, if, through some clumsiness on the part of the steers-man, or by the action of the waves, the boat luffs up into the wind's eye, the fore part of the sail between tack and mast is taken aback, and a capsize is then very likely to occur. It is therefore important, if the novice employs this rig, that his tack should be so arranged as to be let go in a second. The author's plan on a lug-rigged boat he once owned was to lead a rope with an iron thimble spliced at the end of it through an eye-bolt in the bows. The tack of the sail was hooked into the thimble, and the rope was made fast to a cleat in the stern sheets, so that it could be cast off in a moment and so send the tack flying out.

But the standing-lug (Fig. 44, p. 126) is a very convenient sail for the amateur boat-sailor. The tack is made fast to the mast, or to the thwart through which the mast passes, and the sail does not require the spritsail rig to be dipped when the boat jibes or goes about. The yard is hooked to a traveller – an iron ring working on the mast, to which the end of the halyard is fastened. A lugsail, in order to stand well, should have a high peak. The smartest lug-sailed open pleasure-boats are to be found on the Clyde, and among them are some very fast racers. In these boats the main-sheet works on an iron horse, and the halyard is provided with a luff-tackle purchase, so that the sail can be swigged up taut.

A boat rigged with a standing-lug mainsail and mizzen, and a jib, as in Fig. 44, is very handy and safe. If it blows hard the mainsail can be lowered, and the boat can be sailed under mizzen and jib. The mizzen sheet leads through a sheave-hole at the end of the *bumpkin* – as a spar projecting over the stern is called.

Another favourite rig for small boats is the spritsail rig (Fig. 45, p. 127). A spritsail, if well cut and carefully set, stands flatter than a lugsail; for the long spar, or *sprit*, extending diagonally across the sail, prevents it from bagging out. As a rule, the luff of the sail is laced to the mast, but in the larger boats mast-hoops are employed. The tack is fastened to the mast. An iron thimble at the throat of the sail is hooked on to an iron traveller working on the mast and attached to the end of the halyard. The sprit is a spar tapering towards each end; one end fits into an eye at the peak of the sail, and the other end into what is called the *snotter*. The snotter is a short piece of rope with an eye spliced into it at each end; it is passed round the mast, one eye is rove through the other, and the loop thus formed when tightened grips the mast firmly. The end of the sprit fits into the first-mentioned eye.

To set a spritsail, first hoist it; place the upper end of the sprit into the eye at the peak of the sail, and then place the lower end into the eye of the snotter. Lastly, push the snotter up the mast until the sail, standing taut and flat, prevents it going up any further. Wet the snotter if it has a tendency to slip down the mast. In bigger boats the snotter is hoisted and kept in its place by a tackle fitted to the mast, and so cannot slip. It is of the utmost importance that the snotter should be strong, and it should be replaced so soon as it shows any signs of wearing out; for should the snotter, on which there is always a great strain, happen to break when the boat is under way in a breeze, the sprit may be driven through the bottom of the boat. The thing that the skipper of a Thames barge dreads most in bad weather is that his heavy sprit should get adrift and 'take command.'

This is one of the safest of sails. The sprit can be quickly unshipped in a squall, and then the sail blows out a mere flag, offering little resistance to the wind; or again, the sail can be brailed up in a moment to the mast with the brailing-lines – you will see them on every Thames spritsail barge – these lead through blocks on the mast or on the mast-hoops, pass through eyelets in the leach of the sail, and so go right round the sail. On hauling on these lines the sail is snugly furled up along the mast – the most rapid imaginable way of relieving a craft of her canvas until a squall has passed by.

The jib-headed or leg-of-mutton sail, like that represented in Fig. 46 (p. 127), is in some respects the safest of all rigs for a small open boat, and it is very easy to handle. It will be observed that the weight of canvas is mostly in the body of the boat, and that there is very little weight aloft. The sail is laced to the mast, which need be but a light spar, as it has no heavy gaff or yard to support, and small strain comes upon any part of it. One halyard hoists the sail. The sail can be easily rolled up and tied along the mast, or brailing-lines can be employed as in the spritsail-rigged boat.

5

Open Sailing Boats with Boom Sails and Half-Decked Boats

The open-boat rigs described in the last chapter require no booms, and are therefore the safest for the novice's first ventures on the water. A boom much increases the danger of sailing an open boat; even when the sheet is let go a sail bent on a boom holds a great deal of wind, and an accidental jibe in a strong breeze is likely to cause a capsize.

But so soon as the amateur sailor has acquired some experience of seamanship, he will not be content to use sails without booms on his boat. For, as was explained in the last chapter, a sail is rendered far more effective when its foot is extended on a boom. When the boat is running, a sail that has no boom forms into a bag, and does not present its full area to the wind; it cannot be made to stand quite flat even on a wind, and though it jibes with safety, it is more liable to accidental jibes than a sail provided with a boom. Some of the sails described in the last chapter – such as the standing-lug and the leg-of-mutton sail – can be used with or without booms; but with most of the rigs described in this chapter – e.g. the balance-lug and the Una – the boom is indispensable.

The Una Rig, which was introduced to this country from the United States nearly half a century ago, though a somewhat dangerous rig for a novice, has many great advantages. A Una, or cat-rigged boat, as it is termed in America, is certainly the handiest and quickest of boats for turning to windward in narrow waters. The Una boats built on the English coasts – at Cowes or Southampton, for example – are of deeper draught than the orthodox cat-boats of America, and are more comfortable in a choppy sea.

A cat-boat has an almost flat floor. It has very great beam in proportion to its length, the former being in some boats more than half the latter; its deck-plan bears some resemblance to a flat-iron. It therefore has a very light draught. A large cat-boat, in which the author sailed for some months on the coast of Florida, only drew three inches with her centre-board up. The American cat-boat is generally provided with a wooden centre-board; in England an iron centreboard is preferred. The mast is stepped right in the bows, and the one sail, which has a gaff and boom, is shaped as in Fig. 47 (p. 128). The sail is held to the mast either by lacing or by mast-hoops. The sail is hoisted by a single halyard, which, as will be seen on referring to the figure, is made fast to the gaff, leads through a double block on the mast, then through a single block at the jaws of the gaff, then through the double block again, and lastly down the mast to the cleat on deck, to which the fall is fastened. The effect of hauling on the halyard is first to hoist the throat of the sail well up, and then to set up the peak. The boom should always be provided with a topping lift, for unless the boom is topped up it will fall into the water when the sail is lowered, and will dip into it when the boat is running before the wind. Mere skimming-dish though the cat-boat is, her excessive beam gives her great stability, and she can be sailed without any ballast; but, as has already been explained, boats of this class, though stiff up to a particular point, capsize as soon as they have heeled over to a certain angle, and must be sailed with greater care in squally weather than the deep-keeled boats.

The Una, so well adapted for shallow waters, so quick in stays and admirably handy when tacking in narrow channels, would be the ideal boat for single-handed sailing were it not for some serious disadvantages. Being so flat-floored she is uncomfortable in rough water, pounding heavily into the seas and straining herself. Moreover, the weight of her mast, situated, as it is, so far forward, tends to drive her bow into the seas and make her a wet boat on a wind; while she is liable to plunge her nose under and go down by the head when running before a strong squall. The great sail and the length of the boom also make the boat roll when running before the wind; she is then apt to steer very wildly, and is more liable to broach to than a boat of any other rig. It needs a skilled helmsman to steer a cat-boat safely when scudding before a squall in rough water, and a jibe at that juncture would, in all probability, capsize her.

It will be observed that most of the above objections to this rig apply only to its use on rough water. But, unsuitable though the rig may be for open-sea work, it is difficult to beat it on rivers, small lakes, and broads, where there is no room for a sea to rise. As for the other disadvantages of the rig, these can to a great extent be obviated by the following plan adopted by the author on the large cat-boat which he used to sail single-handed in Florida. The waters on which he was cruising were subject to violent squalls and to strong northerly winds, so it was necessary that he should be able to reduce his canvas quickly at times. In the first place, instead of the usual single halyards to which I have referred, he employed two halyards, as in a cutter, throat-halyard and peak-halyard, the former belaying at the foot of the mast, the latter passing through a block at the foot of the mast, and thence leading to a cleat aft within easy reach of the helmsman. He could thus, when a squall struck the boat, let go the peak halyards in a moment without leaving the helm, and so relieve the boat of the pressure of half the sail and the leverage of the great gaff. He might have made her still snugger by having a tricing-tackle fitted to the tack. Then, by hauling the tack up and lowering the peak, the sail would be 'scandalised'. The signification of this last term and a description of a tack tricing-tackle will be found in Chapters 6 and 7. The author also had a balance-reef in the sail – that is, a diagonal reef-band with reef-points, extending from the throat of the sail to the clew.

In order to take in the balance-reef, the jaws of the gaff were lowered to the boom and there made fast. The reef-points were tied round the boom. When the reef was down, the peak was hoisted till the gaff lay along the mast. This left a snug triangular sail, under which the boat would turn to windward in a gale of wind, and, relieved of her top hamper, would run with safety, steering easily, before the heaviest squall.

The sliding-gunter (Fig. 48, p. 128) is the favourite rig of the Bermudas. A boat thus rigged has a very short mast. The sail is of triangular shape, and the upper portion of its luff is laced to a long yard. This yard (see Fig. 49, p. 129) slides up and down the mast on two irons. These irons are fixed to the yard, and are made to work easily on the mast.

The halyards lead through a sheave-hole at the top of the mast, and the end is fastened to the yard at the upper iron, or, better still, passes through an eye on the upper iron, and is made fast at the heel of the yard. The lower portion of the luff of the sail is held to the mast by a lacing. In reefing, the yard is lowered to the required distance; and when the sail is close reefed the end of the yard is brought down to the end of the boom.

This rig, it will be seen, is particularly safe and snug. There is no top hamper and heavy gaff swinging about aloft, and the weight of the sail is in the body of the boat. To let the yard drop and close-reef the sail is a far simpler and quicker process than the reefing of a sail provided with a gaff.

It is well to have a hinge in the lower iron, and to so fit the upper iron that it can be readily unclamped. If the lacing of the lower part of the sail be then cast off, the yard can be lowered on deck, an advantage when at anchor or when it becomes necessary to row the boat against a strong wind.

The sliding-gunter boat generally carries a jib and foresail or one large jib, and sometimes two masts as in the illustration. Like all other rigs, it has some disadvantages, and of these the most serious is the liability of the sliding-irons to jam when the yard is being hoisted or lowered. The irons should therefore be covered with leather, which should always be kept well greased; and a downhaul should be fitted to the end of the yard. It is also a good plan to have the hoops connected by a line on the foreside. This will keep the lower hinged iron in a horizontal position, and much diminish the chances of jamming.

Perhaps the best rig of all for river sailing is the popular balance-lug, so familiar to all those who know the upper Thames. But for rough water it is not a suitable rig. The extreme rigidity of the sail makes it strain the mast a good deal when the boat is in a seaway. There should be plenty of give and take in the gear of a boat that is to toss about on the salt water.

Some boats are rigged with two balance-lugs; others have jibs and mizzens; but for single-handed sailing the most comfortable is the centre-board dinghy with a single balance-lug. Such a boat can be rowed easily, and is yet big enough to carry several passengers. The author is the owner of a boat of this class on the Thames; and a description of her will serve to give an idea of the up-river balance-lug.

This boat (see Fig. 50, p. 129) is built of mahogany; her length is fifteen feet, and her beam five feet. She has an iron centre-board, and her ballast consists of four iron half-hundredweights, two on either side of the centre-board trunk. The lug is laced to a boom and yard, and though a large portion of the sail is before the mast, the sail has not to be dipped when the boat goes about, as is the case with the dipping-lug. It will be observed that the yard has a high peak, and that it is slung at about one-third of its length from its lower end. In many boats of this class the halyard is fastened to an iron mast-traveller, to which the yard is hooked; but one serious objection to this plan is that the sail cannot be fully lowered into the boat until the yard is unhooked from the traveller, or unless the tack and sheet are let go. This is apt to put one in difficulties when one has to lower one's sail hurriedly in a squall; so other methods have been devised for keeping the yard close to the mast, while hoisting the sail by a halyard merely hooked to a thimble on the yard.

One of the best-known of these methods is that adopted by the author on his boat. A line (see Fig. 51, p. 129) is made fast to the yard some inches above the point at which the yard is slung; it then passes round the mast, and leads through an eye on the yard, a foot below the slings. When the sail is set, this line is hauled taut and belayed, thus keeping the yard close to the mast; when the sail lowers, the line slackens and gives the yard free play, so that it can be lowered into the boat. To facilitate the hoisting of the sail the halyard is fitted with a purchase. This will be understood by referring to Fig. 50. It will be seen that at the end of the halyard a block is spliced. A rope is made fast on the mast thwart, and then leading through the block comes down again to form the hauling part. This is a single-whip purchase, and reduces the force to be employed by one-half.

To set a balance-lug sail, the yard is first hoisted to the requisite height with the halyard, and then the tack is hauled down until the sail stands perfectly taut and flat. As considerable force has to be exerted in order to get the tack down, it is usual to have a tack purchase; when the ropes and sail stretch in a breeze, it is by a pull on the tack purchase, and not on the halyards, that the slack is taken in and the sail is made to stand flat again. In the author's boat a luff tackle is employed for the tack; the upper block hooking on to a thimble fastened to the boom, while the lower block hooks on to an eye in the mast. A downhaul is fitted to the yard.

The sheet is thus arranged: One end is fastened to one quarter of the boat; the other end leads through a block on the boom and then through another block fastened to the other quarter.

The mast is supported by a wire stay on either side, and being stepped in what is known as a *tabernacle*, works on a pivot in its heel, so that it can be quickly lowered when a bridge has to be passed under. A rope is spliced into an eye at the lower end of the forestay, passes through a block in the bows, and leads to a cleat aft; when this rope is cast off, the mast comes down without difficulty.

If a balance-lug is properly cut and properly set, it stands flatter than any of the sails hitherto described. The position of the tack, made fast as it is at some distance abaft the fore end of the boom, makes it impossible for the end of the boom to lift in a breeze and for the sail to belly out, as is the case with the standing-lug and other sails. The boom cannot lift without the yard lifting also, and the sail is always perfectly rigid.

It must be allowed that the balance-lug is not an easy sail to handle in squally weather. One cannot reef it without lowering it into the boat; one cannot trice up the tack and lower the peak till the puff is over, as one can with the cat-boat; one cannot brail it up as one can the spritsail. But with all these disadvantages it is, when skilfully handled, the best rig for the river.

The main and mizzen is a favourite rig for balance-lug canoes and small boats, and it is no doubt a very handy one. Sometimes the mizzen-bumpkin is fastened on to the rudder head and so moves with it. The result is that in tacking, when the helm is put down, the mizzen is forced to windward and helps the boat round. This plan, which is adopted on the Thames sailing-barges, will certainly prevent a clumsy boat from missing stays; but the mizzen becomes a back sail every time the boat goes about, and must stop her way to some extent. Moreover, with the mizzen so arranged the helmsman dares not leave his tiller for a moment, for if he does so the wind pressing on the mizzen forces the rudder down, and the boat falls off before the wind (at the risk of capsizing if the breeze is strong), instead of luffing up into it, as all open sailing-boats should do when left to themselves.

The main and mizzen rigged boat in Fig. 52 (p. 130) has wooden battens in her two lugs after the Chinese fashion. With the assistance of battens a sail attains the maximum of flatness. The battens do not materially increase the weight of the sail, as they are made of light deal. They are passed through the reef bands of the sail. The dotted lines in the diagram indicate their position. This rig is peculiarly adapted for single-handed sailing; for a very large sail can be carried with safety if it be provided with battens, as reefing becomes an exceedingly simple and almost instantaneous process. To take in a reef, the halyard is slacked off a sufficient length; and then a pull on a line, which is rove through thimbles fastened at both ends of the batten and boom, draw boom and lower batten close together, and the reef is down, for the reef points need not be tied. The other reefs can be taken down in the same way. In squally weather reefs can be taken in and shaken out half a dozen times in a minute if necessary. Of course, if one has time to do so one will tie the reef-points, as the reef will then be snugger.

The sloop rig (Fig. 53, p. 130) is well adapted for sea work, but is not a handy rig for single-handed sailing if the sailor be a novice; for the tending of the jib-sheets when tacking gives the helmsman more work than he may care for on a windy day. The sloop is rigged much like the cutter; its mainsail, like the cutter's, has a boom and gaff and is hoisted by two halyards, the throat and peak halyards; but whereas the cutter has a forestay fixed to the stem, carries two head-sails, a jib and foresail, and has a bowsprit that can be reefed and drawn inboard, the sloop has a fixed bowsprit or bumpkin, to the end of which the forestay is carried, and for head-sail has but one large jib. A topsail can be carried on a sloop as on a cutter, and a spinnaker can be used for running before the wind. As the running and standing rigging of a sloop is practically the same as that of a cutter, it is unnecessary to describe it in this chapter.

If the mainsail of a small boat – whether she be cat-boat, balance-lug, or sloop – have a boom, it is usual to have the foot of the sail laced to the boom instead of having it secured at the two extremities only, as is often the case with the cutter's mainsail. A sail thus laced undoubtedly stands flatter, and as the lacing distributes the strain along the boom, that spar need not be so stout and heavy as it would have to be with a sail that was not laced.

I have already pointed out that the different sorts of open sailing-boats I have described are often provided with jibs and mizzens. For river and smooth water sailing the single-handed sailor had best confine himself to one sail; it is difficult to see what advantage he can gain by having more. Even if he decide to carry a mizzen as well as a mainsail in his boat, he should at any rate abjure the jib, always a troublesome sail to work in narrow waters. The boat with the single sail is not only the handiest, but it is the fastest; that is, given a certain area of canvas, that canvas is far more effective if it be all put into one sail than if it be divided into several sails; and this is more especially the case when a boat is on a wind. It is only because huge sails are difficult to handle that seagoing vessels have so many sails – an objection that does not apply to small boats.

But when a boat is intended for cruising on choppy waters it is inadvisable to fit her with one big sail, which also involves a lofty mast. When tumbling about in a seaway in a strong breeze the less top hamper the better, so that a smaller mainsail and a jib constitute the best rig. When running or sailing with the wind abeam, a boat is more easy to steer if she has a jib; a boat with one sail is apt to miss stays if the sea is rough, but with the assistance of a jib her head can always be paid off.

On some small craft, which, like the sloop, carry one head-sail only, the foot of the jib is laced to the boom, which makes the sail stand much flatter, more especially when the boat is sailing free and the sheet is slacked off.

There is also a convenient plan by which the head-sail can be used as jib or spinnaker at will. The after end of the bowsprit is fitted to an iron gooseneck on the mast which allows it to work freely in all directions. The bowsprit does not pass through a gammon iron, neither is it otherwise fixed to the stem of the boat, but has attached to it a line or out-haul which is rove through an eyebolt in the stem and is then led aft to a belaying cleat. When the sail is to serve as jib, this line is hauled taut and belayed; this brings the spar amidships, and it acts as a bowsprit. When one is running before the wind the line is slacked off, and by means of one of the two guys attached to the end of it the spar is swung round, on the gooseneck as pivot, to the required side, until it is at right angles to the length of the boat; it then becomes spinnaker-boom, and the sail serves as spinnaker, one of the jib-sheets now acting as spinnaker tack.

On many small craft carrying a single head-sail the latter is conveniently reefed by an arrangement that reefs it along the forestay.

As has already been pointed out, it is better that a small boat, intended for single-handed sailing and rowing on smooth water, should be entirely open; decking of any description is for her unnecessary, is much in the way, and adds to the weight. But with a slightly bigger craft, intended for cruising on more exposed waters, where one is likely to fall in with a lumpy sea at times, it is of advantage to have a half deck. A half-decked boat can be sailed with greater safety in rough water than if she were quite open; a sudden heeling of the boat, that would at once fill and swamp an open boat, will only send the water flowing down the lee waterways, leaving the half-decked boat dry within. A half-decked boat (Fig. 54, p. 131) is partly decked fore and aft, and has waterways on either side. The well is surrounded by a low coaming to keep the water out. In the bigger half-decked boats the deck forward covers a cuddy or small cabin which affords comfortable sleeping quarters, while spacious lockers, in which sails, stores, and so forth can be stowed away, surround the sides of the well and occupy the space under the after-deck.

In addition to the rigs described in this chapter as suitable for small craft, there are others with which I have not dealt as being not in use in this country. There is the lateen-rig, for example, graceful, but somewhat difficult to manage, and having the disadvantages of the standing-lug. The account of two cruises in lateen-rigged craft with which this volume ends will convey some idea of the Arab method of handling their vessels.

6

Decked Boats

So soon as the small-boat sailor has gained his experience, he will in all probability be anxious to own a yacht with which he can cruise with comfort and safety on the open sea; and this he can certainly do with a ten-tonner, or an even smaller craft, provided she be a good sea-boat, and sound in hull and gear from truck to keel. As we are now concerned with small craft only, of ten tons and under, nothing need be said of the schooner rig, which is only suitable for larger vessels; and it will suffice to give in this chapter a description of the spars, sails, standing and running rigging of the cutter, the favourite English rig for this class of boat, and to make some remarks on the yawl and ketch rigs which but slightly differ from that of the cutter.

Within a few feet of the head of the mast (see Fig. 56, p. 132) are, *a,* the *hounds,* projecting wooden shoulders which support the shrouds and stays, and if the vessel have a topmast, the hounds are surmounted by what is termed *the yoke.* The yoke, *b,* is made of hard wood and is strengthened by an encircling iron band; the yoke fits round the mast and is bolted to it.

The topmast is made to slide through the *cap, c,* an iron ring fastened to the fore end of the masthead, and also through a hole in the fore side of the yoke. When hoisted, it is kept in its place by the *fid, d,* a short iron bar which, passing through a hole at the heel of the topmast, rests on the yoke, and prevents the spar from coming down. Contrivances have been invented by which the topmast can be fidded and unfidded, and so can be sent up or brought down from the deck, without its being necessary to send a hand aloft, a great advantage on a small boat. The topmast should work easily, but not too loosely, through the yoke and cap, and so should the fid through the hole in the spar; for it is important that a topmast should come down quickly. In heavy weather a vessel is relieved to an extraordinary extent when this spar, whose weight aloft exerts enormous leverage, is housed on deck. To the yoke also are fitted the cross-trees (see Fig. 56, p. 132, *e),* over which the topmast shrouds are carried to give them further spread. At the head of the topmast is the truck, *8,* a wooden cap through which the signal halyards are rove.

The bowsprit (Fig. 57, p. 133) is made to run in and out easily. It passes between strong wooden bits *a,* which are securely fastened to the deck, and then through the *gammon iron, b,* an iron ring covered with leather which is bolted on the stem head. When the bowsprit is run out, it is kept in its place by an iron fid, *c,* which passes through the bowsprit heel, and rests against the foreside of the bitts. It is usual to have two or three fid holes in the bowsprit, so that the spar can be run in and reefed to the required length according to the jib that is to be set. To shorten the bowsprit in bad weather relieves the vessel quite as much as does the housing of the topmast; for the great leverage exercised by this long overhanging spar tends to drive the vessel's bows into the seas. It is therefore important that the bowsprit should come in readily. The gammon iron should be large; and the fid should be stout, else the strain on it may cause it to bend, and so to jam.

The boom is usually fitted to the mast with a galvanised-iron gooseneck, giving it free play in every direction. When a yacht is sailing, the mainsail exerts a great strain upon the boom, so that unless it is sufficiently stout the spar buckles, or bends, and the sail can no longer stand flat. The chief strain comes upon the centre of the boom, so that it is always made thicker in that part and is tapered away towards either end.

The weight of a cutter's boom, and the leverage of its great length always acting on the lee-side, and so diminishing the stability of the vessel, become a source of danger in a heavy sea, causing the vessel to labour and strain; one of the most serious accidents that can befall a cutter when combating a gale is for this unwieldy spar to get adrift, or carry away and 'take command', when it is not unlikely to drive a hole through the vessel's side, or to sweep the crew off the deck. Thus it is that the prudent captain of the cutter in heavy weather stows his mainsail, lashes his boom amidships, and sails under his snug trysail.

With the object of reducing the weight of the boom as much as possible, while leaving it sufficiently stiff to resist the strain of the sail without buckling, hollow and built spars have been employed on large cutters. The prejudice that so long existed in England as to the undesirability of lacing the foot of the mainsail to the boom has almost disappeared. It has dawned upon us that this practice, universally adopted in America, does not necessarily destroy the springiness and liveliness of a vessel, and so make her a worse sea-boat and a slower sailer. That a mainsail stands flatter when bent to the boom is beyond question. Moreover, another most important advantage is gained, as has been pointed out in a previous chapter; a far lighter boom will resist the strain of the sail without buckling, when lacing is employed, than when the sail is merely attached to the two extremities of the spar.

The gaff, like the boom, should be no heavier than is absolutely necessary. A heavy gaff, when hoisted, involves excessive top hamper, a weight aloft exerting great leverage, all of which is directed so as to decrease the stability of the vessel, and make her labour in a seaway. But, on the other hand, the gaff must not be too light, else it will buckle in a breeze, and the sail will be baggy.

The gaff travels up and down the mast on the jaws. These are horns of wood or iron covered with leather. The latter are neater, and are not so likely to jam the halyards. The jaws half encircle the mast, and the parral, a line with wooden beads threaded on it, passes round the mast from one horn of the jaws to the other, and so prevents the jaws from losing their hold on the mast.

The topsail yard is a light spar, to which the head of the topsail is bent, and to which the topsail halyards are made fast.

We now come to the cutter's sails. These are the mainsail, the foresail, the jib, and the topsail. The upper edge of a sail is called the head; the fore or weather edge is the luff; the lower edge is the foot; and the after edge is the leach. The different corners of the sails also have their names: the upper fore corner is the throat of the sail; the upper after comer is the peak; the lower fore corner is the tack; and the lower after corner is the clew. Of these sails the mainsail and the foresail alone are provided with reef-points, 9, and reef-cringles, 10, so that their area can, when necessary, be reduced by taking in one or more reefs, a process that will be explained further on. Instead of reefing a jib when the wind freshens, the sail is taken in and a smaller jib is hoisted in its stead; for every cutter should carry at least two jibs, and it is better to have three, even on a five-tonner – one being a very small spit-fire jib of stout canvas, to be used if one is caught out in really heavy weather. Larger yachts carry five or six jibs. In strong winds the topsail is taken in, and the topmast is housed; or a small jib-headed topsail is hoisted in the place of the yard topsail.

The mainsail has its head laced to the gaff, and its foot, as has been said, is sometimes laced to the boom. Its luff is fastened to the wooden or iron mast hoops that are made to run easily up and down the mast. On a large vessel the clew of the mainsail is hauled out on the boom by a tackle, and the tack also is hauled down by the main-tack tackle; but on small vessels a rope is spliced into the thimble in the tack of the sail and made fast to the boom; while the clew is hauled out by hand with a line rove through a hole at the end of the boom. But this clew outhaul should never be so fastened that it cannot be easily cast-off; for it should be tautened when one goes out sailing, and slackened up when one returns to one's moorings. If it is made a fixture, as is too often done, it becomes much too taut after a shower of rain has shrunk the sail and ropes, and is certain to pull the sail out of shape.

The foresail in a cutter is the triangular sail set in the forestay; along the luff of the sail are attached at intervals hanks or iron hoops, which run up and down the forestay. It can be reefed down like the mainsail.

The jib is a triangular sail whose clew is hauled out on the bowsprit. It was the old fashion to have the cloths of this sail parallel with the leach. But a jib thus cut has a tendency to get very baggy, in which case it is always on the shake, and becomes ineffective when the vessel is close-hauled. On nearly all cutter yachts, what are known as angulated jibs are now used, in which half the cloths are parallel with the foot of the sail and the other half parallel with the leach (Fig. 58, p. 134). A jib thus constructed stands very flat.

The yard topsail is laced to the yard. The jib topsail is a triangular sail, whose luff is laced to the mast after it is hoisted. On a very small yacht it is well to dispense with a topmast, and carry what is known as a pole-mast, that is, a mast which is prolonged above the hounds in a long tapering pole. A yard topsail can be set on a pole-mast in the following manner. The sail is stretched out on the deck and its luff is laced to a light yard (see Fig. 59, p. 134). The halyard is bent on to the yard at *a,* and passes through a sheave-hole in the mast; the sail is then hoisted till it is chock-a-block, the halyard is belayed, and the yard is made to lie straight up and down the mast by means of a down-haul, *b,* fastened to the heel of the spar. The sail is sheeted aft to the gaff like the ordinary topsail. In order to set a larger topsail without increasing the hoist, a jack-yard, *c,* is often employed. This is a small spar, bent on the after end of a topsail's foot, which extends the sail to some distance beyond the end of the gaff. The spinnaker is a large jib-headed sail of light canvas only used for running before the wind, when it is boomed out on the opposite side to the mainsail. The spinnaker-boom works on a gooseneck on the foreside of the mast, and, when not in use, is generally topped up so as to lie along the mast. On large yachts the spinnaker-boom, when topped up, rises above the hounds, so that it has always to be unshipped for a jibe. It is more convenient on a small cruising yacht to have a shorter boom that will dip under the forestay, and can therefore be passed over to the other side without being unshipped. In Fig. 60 (p. 134)a cutter is represented sailing before the wind with spinnaker set. In Fig. 60, *a* is the gooseneck on the mast to which the spinnaker-boom, *b,* is attached; *c* is the topping lift which supports the boomwhen the spinnaker is set, and by means of which the boom is topped up along the mast; *d* is the after-guy, which is fastened to the spinnaker boom and leads aft. It enables the boom to be trimmed to the required angle. It is also advisable to have a fore-guy, leading from the boom to the bows to prevent the spinnaker from jibing accidentally, or from swinging aft when the yacht is rolling about on a swell in a very light breeze, *e* is the spinnaker-halyard passing through a block fastened on the mast; *f* is the out-haul by which the sail is hauled out on the boom; *g* is the sheet which is made fast on deck.

Every cruising yacht should carry a trysail for use in heavy weather. This is a small sail with a short head and gaff (some trysails are jib-headed and have no gaff). The trysail is set in the place of the mainsail; it has no boom, and has two sheets, which are generally luff-tackles, one leading to each quarter. The luff of the sail is laced to the mast.

We now come to the cutter's standing and running rigging. Whereas the running rigging, consisting of the halyards, sheets, etc., which are employed for the hoisting and trimming of the sails, have constantly to be handled during the manoeuvring of a vessel, the standing rigging, consisting of the shrouds, stays, and so forth, is permanently fixed, or, at any rate, has to be shifted but occasionally, its object being to support the mast and bowsprit, and to prevent them from yielding to the pressure of the wind.

Wire standing rigging is employed even on the smallest boats, and its superiority to hemp rigging is now unquestioned. To commence with the rigging of the cutter's mast, it is supported on either side by two wire shrouds. On larger vessels three or four shrouds a side are used, and the small lines known as ratlines are fastened across them to form the rungs of a rudder. At the upper end of each shroud an eye is spliced, which is passed over the head of the mast and rests on the hounds. To the lower end of each shroud a deadeye is attached by an eye-splice. (A deadeye is a wooden block with three holes in it.) On the chain-plates, *13*, are attached other deadeyes, corresponding in number to those on the shrouds, and the rigging is set up by lanyards, ropes which are rove backwards and forwards between the two sets of deadeyes, in the fashion familiar to every one who has seen a sailing-vessel.

On very small yachts deadeyes are usually dispensed with, and a line, with one end of it spliced to the eye in the shroud, and passing several times through that eye and another eye on the chain-plates, is all that is required.

Iron screws are also sometimes employed instead of rope lanyards, but it is difficult to get over one's prejudice against these – if it be a prejudice – for one would imagine that thus to rigidly pin down a mast with iron, and so allow it no play, must put an unfair strain on the chain-plates and the sides of the vessel.

Next we have that important support to the mast, the forestay, *H*, also of stout wire. Its eye is passed over the masthead after the shrouds have been put in their place, and it rests on the top of these. It is generally led over the stem, and is passed back to the deck through a hole in the stem head. An eye is spliced in its end, and is set up by a lanyard to a strong ring-bolt in the deck or to the bowsprit bitts. The iron hoops, to which the luff of the foresail is bent, are threaded on the forestay.

The mainmast is further stayed by the runners, *15*, a great support when the vessel is running before the wind. The runners are set up by tackle; it is always necessary, when sailing, that whichever one becomes the lee runner should be quickly slacked off so as to allow the main boom to swing sufficiently far out.

To support the topmast, we have first the topmast shrouds, *16*; these are spread out by the cross-trees, as has already been explained, and lead down to the chain-plates. When running before the wind, preventer backstays, *17*, are also used. They are set up with a tackle and can be cast off easily; for to allow the boom free play, the lee one must be let go, and it must not be forgotten that an accidental jibe, with the preventer backstay standing, will probably carry away the topmast.

The topmast stay, *18,* leading from the topmast head to the end of the bowsprit, gives an additional support to the topmast. When a jib topsail is used, its luff is fastened to hanks which run up and down the topmast stay.

The bowsprit is stayed by the bobstay and the bowsprit shrouds; the bobstay, *18a,* is the stay underneath the bowsprit which prevents it from lifting; on a vessel of ten tons it would be arranged as follows. A piece of wire rope is shackled on to the stem close to the water line; to this is attached a rope tackle with a single block at the lower end and a double block at its upper end, the double block being shackled on the cranse iron at the bowsprit end. This tackle is known as a luff-tackle purchase, for small yachts a tackle of two single blocks would suffice (a gun-tackle purchase). In either case the fall of the bobstay tackle leads from the double block, along the bowsprit, and is belayed on deck, generally on the bowsprit bitts. The cranse mentioned above is the iron cap or hoop, with eyes on to which all the bowsprit rigging is hooked – one eye underneath for the bobstay, one on each side for the shrouds, and one at the top for the topmast stay.

The bowsprit shrouds are also of wire rope. The method of fitting them will be made clear by referring to Fig. 57 (p. 133). At one end they are shackled on to the cranse iron; and to the other end are attached rope tackles, *d.* In small vessels the tackles are hooked to eyebolts on the outside of the vessel, the falls leading inboard through holes cut for them in the bulwarks; but a better plan is that adopted on the larger yachts, of having the whole tackle brought on board; if the blocks are overboard, they drag through the water and stop the vessel's way when she leans over to the wind. In order to give the bowsprit shrouds more spread and so make them more effective, they are sometimes extended by whiskers, *e,* iron rods fitted to the stem head, and terminating in little iron jaws on which the shrouds can run easily.

When a bowsprit is reefed, both bobstay and bowsprit shrouds have to be tautened up by taking in the slack of the tackle. A small line is attached to the bobstay so that it can be hauled up out of the way – the tackle having been first slacked off to a sufficient extent – when the vessel is lying at anchor.

RUNNING RIGGING

We now come to the cutter's running rigging; and to commence with the mainsail, we find that it is hoisted by two sets of halyards, the throat halyards and the peak halyards. The throat halyards of a small vessel would probably consist of a luff-tackle purchase, the single block being hooked on to an eyebolt at the throat of the gaff, and the double block on to the after-side of the mast close to the hounds. On larger vessels a more powerful purchase would, of course, be employed. The fall of the throat halyards leads down the starboard side of the mast and is belayed to the mast bitts; these are stout upright timbers securely bolted through the deck into the deck-beams, and having cross pieces attached to them with racks for belaying-pins.

In larger vessels purchases are fitted to the standing parts of throat, peak, jib, and other halyards in order to obtain greater power. The purchase consists of two blocks, of which one is sometimes a double block; the lower block of the purchase is hooked on to an eyebolt on the deck near the foot of the mast. When a vessel is under way it is far easier to get the sails taut by swinging on the purchases than by hauling on the halyards. Purchases are not required for small craft except for racing purposes. The less gear the better on the miniature yacht, and if you have too many halyards, purchases, and what not dangling along your mast, your amateur crew are likely to get very confused and to be ever hauling at or letting go the wrong rope. A friend of mine, who had never been at sea before, but who volunteered to join me on a cruise round the world on my thirty-ton yawl the *Falcon,* exclaimed in dismay when he first beheld her, 'Oh, what a lot of strings there are about this boat! I shall never know the use of them all.' And he never did master the ropes, though he was a volunteer hand on board for several months and sailed over many thousands of miles of ocean. The small sailing-boat needs but few 'strings', but too often her owner over 'strings' her and over blocks her, under the impression that she thus has a more imposing and yachtlike appearance.

The peak halyards, by which the peak of the mainsail is hoisted, are rove through single blocks on the gaff and on the masthead, the number of the blocks depending on the size of the sail. The peak halyards are such as would be used on a 10-ton cutter. The fall leads through the lower block on the mast, down the port side of the mast, to be belayed on the mast bitts. The standing part leads through the upper block and is then fastened to the peak purchase, which is fitted in the same way as the throat purchase. If no peak purchase is used there is no upper block on the mast, and the standing part of the halyard is hooked on an eyebolt at the masthead.

The tack tricing line is used to haul up the tack of the mainsail. This relieves a vessel considerably when caught in a squall, and also enables the man at the helm to see better ahead and avoid other vessels when sailing into a crowded harbour. One objection to the lacing of a mainsail to the boom is that the tack of the sail cannot be triced up unless the lacing is cast off.

On small craft the tack tricing line is made fast to the tack of the sail, passes through a block under the gaff close to the jaws, and then leads down the mast to the deck. The main tack, which, as has already been said, is on small vessels merely a rope spliced into the tack cringle and belayed to the boom gooseneck, must of course be cast off before the corner of the sail can be triced up. The tack tricing line also serves as a throat downhaul when the mainsail is being lowered. In larger craft the tack is triced up by a gun-tackle purchase with one single block at the tack of the sail and another under the throat of the gaff.

A small cutter's mainsheet should always work on an iron horse as in Fig. 61 (p. 135). A horse keeps the boom down, and obviates that lifting of the spar, and consequent bellying out of the sail which occurs when the mainsheet is otherwise fitted. A main-sheet, arranged as in Fig. 61, is suitable for a small yacht.

One end of the sheet is spliced round a single block which works on the horse; the sheet is rove through a double block stropped on to the boom, through the single block, back again through the double block, and lastly, through a block on the deck amidships, from which it is led to the cleat on which it is belayed.

On either side of the sail are the topping lifts, two stout ropes, which, when hauled taut, relieve the sail of the weight of the boom, and are of especial service when the vessel is running before the wind. The standing part of a topping-lift is hooked on to an eye in an iron band encircling the boom; the hauling part is rove through a single block on the hounds of the mast and then leads down the mast to terminate in a purchase similar to that used for the throat halyards.

The peak downhaul is a line leading through a single block at the gaff end. It is used for hauling down the peak when the mainsail is being lowered. On small crafts it also serves as the ensign halyards.

We next come to the running rigging of the foresail. Even on large yachts no purchase is fitted to the standing part of the fore halyards; for as the sail is set on a stay, its luff being attached to the hanks which work on the forestay, it needs but little power to haul it taut. On a ten-tonner the fore halyards are generally fitted as follows. The standing part is hooked on to an eyebolt on one side of the masthead under the yoke, then the rope is led through a single block hooked on to the cringle at the head of the sail, passes up again to be rove through a single block hooked on to an eyebolt under the yoke (on the opposite side of the mast to that on which the eyebolt for the standing part is fixed), and then leads down the mast to its belaying-pin.

On a small cutter the tack cringle of the foresail is usually hooked on to the stern; but on larger vessels a tack tackle is employed.

The foresheets are fitted in various ways. The method shown in Fig. 62 (p. 135) will do well for a small yacht. Two single blocks are hooked on to the clew of the foresail. The standing part of each sheet is spliced into an eye on deck; the other end is rove through one of the single blocks on the clew, and leads to the cleat aft to which it is to be belayed. In the diagram the sheets are also led through two blocks fastened to the deck of the boat; this is a good plan – it enables the sail to be hauled in flat to the most effective angle, and also makes the labour easier. In larger vessels the standing part of each foresheet is stropped to one of the single blocks hooked on to the clew, is rove through a single block fastened to the deck or bulwarks about abreast of the mast, then back through the block on the clew of the sail, and thence aft to its belaying-pin.

On a small yacht the jib halyards are fitted in exactly the same way as the fore halyards. They are rove through a single block, which is hooked or shackled on to the head of the sail; the eyebolt to which the standing part of the halyards is hooked, and the upper block through which they lead, are on opposite sides of the mast, above the yoke, close under the masthead. On all large vessels a jib purchase is fitted to the standing part of the jib halyards.

The tack of the jib is hooked on to an iron traveller, a hoop working easily on the bowsprit. The traveller is then hauled out to the bowsprit end by the jib out-haul which is thus fitted. One end of a rope is spliced into an eye on the traveller, and the other end is rove through a sheave-hole at the bowsprit end just inside the cranse iron. The rope enters the sheave-hole from above, and coming out beneath, has a single block spliced into its end. Another rope is rove through this block, one end of the rope being made fast to the bowsprit bitts or to some other convenient place, while the other end leads on board to form the hauling part. A small line should be fastened to the traveller to lead on board and serve as in-haul.

The jib sheets of a very small vessel do not require tackle; but they should be led through fairleads or blocks so situated that they bring the sail down to the most effective angle when the vessel is close-hauled, and prevent it from bellying. Knots should be tied at the ends of both jib and fore sheets, so that in case they get adrift they will not slip through the blocks or fairleads.

Lastly, we have the running rigging connected with the topsail. The topsail halyards of a small cutter consist of a single rope which is rove through a sheave-hole at the head of the topmast, close under the topmast rigging.

The topsail sheet, see Fig. 59 (c), is rove through a sheave-hole at the end of the gaff and through a block on a wire pendant, fastened on to the jaws of the gaff. This is the plan adopted, whether the topsail be a yard topsail or a jib header. The tack is led down and belayed at the foot of the mast.

The rig of the yawl, or dandy, differs but slightly from that of the cutter. The yawl's boom does not project over the counter as does the cutter's, and the mainsail is accordingly smaller than that of the single stick boat. The yawl, see Fig. 63 (p. 136), carries a small mizzen-mast or jigger on her counter, which enables her to set a little mizzen-sail, generally either a standing-lug or a leg-of-mutton sail. A short outrigger or bumpkin may be fitted to a yawl's stern, at the end of which is a block or sheave-hole through which the mizzen-sheet is rove. If the mizzen is a good sized one, the bumpkin is provided with wire shrouds leading to either side of the stern, and with a wire bobstay. The mizzen-mast generally has one wire shroud on each side. Sometimes the mizzen-mast is further supported by stays leading from the masthead forward, which are set up by tackles. These stays are not used when the vessel is sailing free; the weather one is set up when the vessel is close-hauled. Care must be taken to ease off the tackle if the main boom is swinging over, else it may carry away the mizzen.

A yawl is not so fast as a cutter of the same size, but she is far more easily handled, and is much to be preferred for single-handed cruising. Having a shorter and lighter boom, she is more fitted to encounter heavy weather; as the boom is all inboard, it is easy to take in reefs in the mainsail; whereas to reef down the large mainsail of a cutter yacht, on an unwieldy boom projecting far over the counter, is a difficult and laborious task when the vessel is tumbling about in a seaway.

A yawl, too, can be comfortably hove to under mizzen and jib, and then, if there be but one man on board, he can leave the helm while he lowers the mainsail on deck and reefs it at his leisure, the vessel taking care of herself.

Moreover, the operation of reefing, necessarily of so frequent occurrence on a cutter, can often be avoided on a yawl; when the rising wind demands the reduction of canvas, this can be done by other methods than reefing, while yet leaving the sails nicely balanced. For example, when struck by a squall a vessel can be greatly relieved by hauling down the foresail. But to lower the foresail of a cutter without at the same time reefing the mainsail puts the vessel out of trim, causes her to carry excessive weather helm, and in some cases to become almost unmanageable. On a yawl, on the other hand, the foresail and mizzen are lowered, and then the vessel will sail well under mainsail and jib. If it comes on to blow still harder, the mainsail can be lowered, and then under mizzen, small jib, and reefed foresail, she will jog along very comfortably.

For knocking about on stormy waters the ketch is to be preferred even to the yawl. This is the snuggest and handiest of all rigs, and is the favourite for our deep-sea fishing-boats and coasters. The ketch (see Fig. 41) like the yawl, has a main and mizzen mast; but the mainsail is smaller and the boom shorter than the yawl's; while the mizzen-mast is not stepped in the counter, but is well inboard, so as just to clear the main boom, and carries a much larger sail than the yawl's mizzen. No mizzen-bumpkin is needed for the sheet, and the mizzen-boom works on a horse on the counter. The mizzen-mast is rigged like the mainmast with shrouds and runners, and also has shifting forestays with tackles. The mizzen-sail has a gaff like the mainsail, its luff is fastened to mast-hoops, it is hoisted by throat and peak halyards, and a jib-headed topsail is often set above it. I cruised for two summers on the Baltic on a ketch of three tons register; and, remembering that experience, were I ever again to fit out a small vessel for an ocean voyage, I would certainly – more especially if my crew was composed of amateurs – adopt this very safe and handy rig, even though it were at the expense of a little speed.

The yawl and ketch require fewer hands to handle them than the cutter. Thus, when I visited the desert island of Trinidade with my fifty-six tonner, the Alerte, the majority of my companions were encamped on shore, digging for the treasure which was never found; while two of us only remained on board to look after the yacht, which, in consequence of the badness of the anchorage, was ever kept under weigh on the open Atlantic. For months, in fair weather and foul, we two were thus afloat. By night we used to heave her to, some miles off the shore, under trysail and small jib, and in the morning we used to hoist the foresail and sail in towards the shore to communicate with our friends by signal (for the perpetual heavy surf made landing dangerous and often impossible). We even sailed her thus short-handed to Bahia and back to obtain provisions – a voyage of fourteen hundred miles. We should have had a good deal more difficulty in doing this had our vessel been cutter-rigged.

7

Seamanship

Having described the various portions of the rigging of a small fore-and-aft craft, I will now explain how the principal manoeuvres connected with the sailing of the boat are executed. Practice alone will enable the amateur sailor to promptly decide what course of action he should take in any set of conditions that may arise, and to perform the required operations smartly and without hesitation. For that 'he who hesitates is lost' is an adage that has but too often been proved true at sea. The sailor must be able to put his hands upon any rope on board, in a moment, in the darkest night; and to reef, tie, or untie any knot, as well with his eyes shut as open. But the novice must not be discouraged if he make mistakes at first. All novices commit strange blunders when orders are given them to do this or that, as the two following anecdotes will show. It is now several years ago that I sailed from Southampton on a thirty-ton yacht with a crew of amateurs, of whom only one had ever before in his life handled tiller or hauled on rope at sea. It was a crew of briefless barristers, by the way, and people prophesied that with such a strange ship's company we should never get outside the chops of the Channel. However, we contrived to reach Buenos Ayres, and to cruise over many thousands of miles of the South Atlantic Ocean without mishap. My companions, with the exception of the one who took the port watch, did not even know the names of the ropes before starting, and their nautical education commenced when we weighed our anchor.

I took the starboard watch with one of the briefless barristers, and this is what occurred one stormy night in mid-Atlantic. I quote the description of the incident from *The Cruise of the Falcon*, the published narrative of the voyage: 'Time, 2 A.M. Dark and squally night. Captain steering. A smoking and pondering (supposed to be looking out). Captain, observing squall coming up, loquitur: "A, just run forward and scandalise the mainsail, will you? Begin by tricing up the tack."

'A creeps deliberately forward, and disappears in the darkness. Five minutes elapse. Captain, impatiently: "Now, then, have not you finished that yet?"

'A: "In a minute – in a minute."

'Another five minutes elapse; we are now in the middle of the squall, which does not prove so violent as was anticipated. Captain, very impatient: "You are a nice, useful fellow on board a yacht! Ten minutes, and you have not triced up that tack. If that had been a serious squall, we might have gone to the devil while you were fiddling about there."

'A (very indignant): "I do not care. I will leave the beastly thing alone. I will not be sworn at. In the daytime I can find the strings; in the night I cannot, and I shall no longer try."'

So, too, on another occasion, when it was my watch below, I was awakened by a tremendous row, a banging about of ropes, and louder, above the din, the stentorian voice of the officer of the watch raised in anger. On coming on deck I found that, on being ordered to let fly the jib-sheet, that the ship might go about, the briefless barrister on that watch had let go in succession the jib halyards, the bowsprit shrouds, and the peak halyards. And with this crew the Falcon was navigated across the Atlantic and half round the world! So there is hope for the clumsiest tyro.

Before explaining how the different manoeuvres are performed on a yacht, I will describe how the sails are hoisted, lowered, and reefed.

The mainsail, when stowed in harbour, is rolled up neatly, the middle of the leach having been first hauled forward and laid along the boom. When the sail is furled, its folds are tied together by short lengths of rope, or canvas strips, called tyers or gaskets. The sail is then covered with a coat of painted canvas, which is laced underneath the boom; but the coat should never be put on unless the sail is thoroughly dry, else mildew will soon make its appearance. The boom when the sail is furled rests on a wooden crutch.

To set the mainsail. Remove the sail-coat; hook on the peak halyards; slack off the main-sheet, so as to allow the boom to be topped up a few feet with the topping-lift – if there are two topping-lifts, haul on the weather one; then get the main-sheet taut again, and belay it; cast off the tyers. The sail is now ready for hoisting. To get it up, haul on both throat and peak halyards until the throat is as high as it will go and the luff of the sail is drawn taut; but while doing this do not let the peak of the sail get higher than the throat, for if the peak be hoisted too fast the throat will travel up the mast with difficulty, and cannot be got taut. Take care also that the gaff passes between the two topping-lifts, or on the right side of the single topping-lift, if there be but one topping-lift, as is usual on small cutters. The throat being well up, belay the throat halyards; then haul away on the peak halyards until the peak is well up – that is, until the sail begins to wrinkle at the throat.

In order to get the sail to stand as flat as possible, the tack should be made fast before hoisting.

If the clew of the sail has not been hauled out taut along the boom before the sail is hoisted, this should be done before the peak is right up, and before the tack is fast.

When the sail is up, stow away in a locker, or other place set apart for the purpose, the boom-crutch, mainsail-coat, and tyers; for nothing is more unseamanlike than to leave lying about on deck gear which is not required for immediate use. 'Where the dickens have those other two tyers got to?' 'I don't know, Ted. They must have been washed overboard when we shipped that sea,' is the sort of conversation, over the stowing of a sail after a cruise, that betokens a slovenly crew.

Having belayed the halyards, coil them neatly, 'with the sun', and then capsize them – that is, turn the coils over, so that the last coil is on the top and the halyard end is underneath. Unless this is done, the halyards, if let go in a hurry, are likely to twist round some of the coils and carry them up the mast, to jam the block and prevent the sail from lowering more than half-way down.

To reef a mainsail. One reef-pennant, or reefearring, at least, should always be kept rove, in readiness for use. A reef-pennant is a rope which passes through a comb-cleat (see Fig. 64, p. 136) at the end of the boom, through the reef-cringle on the sail, and down through a comb-cleat on the opposite side of the boom. The comb-cleat has three reef-holes or more – one for each reef-pennant. At the end of the reef-pennant is a knot which prevents it slipping through the hole in the comb-cleat.

To take a reef down in the mainsail, top up the boom a bit, and haul it well inboard with the sheet; slack away the throat and peak halyards to allow of the reef-cringle being brought down to the boom. When the cringle has been got well down with the earring, secure the earring to the boom with a reef-pennant bend, the method of forming which is shown in the figure. Hook the tack on the reef-cringle at the luff of the sail, bowse it down and secure it. Roll up the foot of the sail tightly, and tie the reef-points as taut as possible; then haul on the halyards till the sail is once more properly set.

To scandalise a mainsail. So as to reduce the area of canvas rapidly in a squall, or as a precaution when about to jibe in a strong wind, the mainsail can be scandalised. This is done by tricing up the tack of the sail with the tricing line and lowering the peak.

To set a jib. In the first place, if they are slack, the bobstay, the bowsprit-shrouds, and the topmast-stay must be hauled taut in succession. Then lay the jib on the deck forward, with its tack turned to the bows. Hook the tack of the sail on the traveller and the halyards to the head-cringle of the sail, not without looking aloft first to see that there are no turns in the halyards. Pass the jib-sheets through the comb-cleats or the leading blocks, and tie an overhand knot at the end of each sheet, to prevent its running out through its fair-lead when the jib is flapping about. Fasten the jib-sheets on to the clew of the sail, and if clip-hooks are employed for this purpose mouse them with twine.

It is usual, when setting a big jib, to first hoist the head of the sail about half-way up with the halyards, then to haul the tack out on the bowsprit, and lastly to hoist the halyards till the sail is right up; but with a small sail it is better to haul the tack out and belay the outhaul fall before pulling on the halyards; for, unless it is blowing hard, it is easy so to handle the sail as to prevent it falling into the water. It is sometimes convenient to hoist a jib without removing the stops – short yarns with which it is tied when rolled up. When the sail is hoisted, a pull on the sheets breaks the yarns and the sail falls out free.

If the jib is being hoisted when the vessel is under way, take the halyards to the lee-side of the foresail before hooking them on to the sail.

To take in a jib, slack up the out-haul and pull the sail inboard, 'muzzling' it – that is, gathering it with your arms as it comes in. Then let go the halyards and pull the sail down. If two hands can be spared for the work, one of them should commence to lower the halyards as the sail is coming in along the bowsprit. It requires an experienced hand to take in a jib smartly in a strong breeze when the boat is tumbling about; and the novice, when undertaking this task single-handed, must be careful not to let the jib blow out of his hands into the water, to tow under the keel.

When the jib is in, unhook the traveller, the sheets, and halyards, and make these all fast in their respective places.

Even on a cutter of considerable tonnage one hand suffices to hoist or lower the foresail. To hoist a foresail, hook the sheets and halyards on the sail, and belay one or both sheets according to circumstances. Then hoist the sail with the halyards and get down the tack – if there is a tack tackle.

To reef a foresail it is best to lower the sail on deck. Roll up the foot of the sail; tie up the reef-point. Hook the tack and sheets to the reef-cringles, and then haul the sail up again with the halyards.

To set a gaff-topsail. Lay the sail on deck and lace its head to the yard. Bend the sheet to the clew with a gaff-topsail sheet-bend (see Fig. 31). Bend on the halyards with a topsail halyard-bend (see Fig. 30). Hoist on the halyards, while keeping some strain on the tack to steady the sail and guide it; and haul in the slack of the sheet as the sail goes up. When the yard is chock-a-block belay the halyards, get the tack down with its tackle and belay it, and lastly haul in the sheet.

To set a jib-headed topsail, a hand is sent aloft who laces the luff of the sail to the topmast while the sail is being hoisted.

The method of setting a jib-headed topsail on a pole mast has already been explained.

Topsails of any sort should be hoisted and lowered on the weather-side of the mainsail. If hoisted or lowered on the lee-side they are apt to blow away. Topsails are passed up between the mainsail and the topping-lift, and care must be taken when bending the sheets to lead them inside the topping-lift.

In order to set a spinnaker, the spinnaker-boom is first lowered to the required side of the vessel by slacking up the spinnaker topping-lift. At the same time the fore and the after guys are led to the two extremities of the vessel, and with these the boom is guided until it has 'squared' – that is, extended overboard at right angles to the keel. The guys are then belayed. The halyards, out-haul, and sheets are bent on to the sail, and the sheet is belayed. The sail is hoisted with the halyards, and then the tack is hauled out to the boom end with the out-haul. If there be much wind it may be found necessary to slack up the sheet a bit until the out-haul has been belayed.

To take in a spinnaker, let go the out-haul first and drag the sail inboard. Then let go the halyards and haul the head of the sail down on deck.

To get under way is not so simple a matter as might be supposed, and is often, indeed, a difficult and delicate business that taxes the skill even of the experienced sailor. 'A slight error of judgment when weighing anchor or slipping from one's moorings in a crowded anchorage may result in one's craft drifting across another vessel's stem, before she can be got under control; and if the tide be running strong, thus to collide with an anchored vessel is likely to cause the sinking of one's own.

Before proceeding to get under way, get whatever sails you intend to use ready for hoisting; cast off their tyers and stops, leaving, perhaps, one tyer round the 'bunt' or middle of the mainsail to keep it from blowing loose; bend on halyards and sheets, top the main boom, and see that the runners, etc., are belayed in their right places.

The usual method of getting under way with a cutter when she is riding head to wind and tide, the wind being moderate, is as follows: Heave short, that is, get up the chain until it is nearly straight up and down, and the yacht is almost over her anchor. Hoist the mainsail. Trip the anchor smartly, and just as it is leaving the ground hoist the jib and foresail; at the same time cant the vessel over on the required tack by putting the helm to port or starboard, as the case may be, for the tide passing under an anchored vessel gives her steerage way, which she preserves for a short time after the anchor is a-weigh. To cant the vessel the quicker, keep the foresail to windward by hoisting it with its weather-sheet belayed (if necessary, keep the jib also to windward), and ease off the main-sheet. As soon as the vessel has paid off sufficiently and her mainsail is filling, let the head-sails draw. If you wish to sail close-hauled, do not flatten in your main-sheet until you have gathered good steerage way. If you wish to run before the wind, ease the main-sheet well off, and you may keep the peak lowered until the vessel's head is well round.

It of course requires two hands to get a vessel under way in the manner described above. But on a small cutter the operation can be performed single-handed. Hoist jib and mainsail before heaving upon the cable, leaving the jib-sheets flowing, but not so loosely that they can get entangled or get foul of the rigging. Heave on the cable; when it is straight up and down flatten in the weather jib-sheet and lash the helm to windward with a line.

Run forward and get the anchor a-trip and on deck as quickly as you are able. Then let draw the jib-sheets, cast off the tiller-line, and sail away. You can get your foresail up as soon as you are clear of other vessels.

If your vessel is riding to tide and wind, and it is blowing hard, hoist no canvas before heaving on the cable, for the pressure of the wind upon the sails would cause the anchor to drag. Just as the anchor is leaving the ground put the helm over to cant the vessel, and hoist the foresail and jib smartly. Hoist the mainsail when the vessel is under way.

If the tide and wind be in opposite directions, and the vessel is riding to the tide with the wind astern, set jib, or jib and foresail, just as the anchor is leaving the ground; you will then be running before the wind; and if you wish to luff quickly have the mainsail up as smartly as you can.

If the wind and tide be in opposite directions, and the wind be so strong that it masters the tide, the vessel riding to the wind with the tide coming up astern, the effect of the rudder will be reversed, so that to cant the vessel's head to port the helm must be put to port, instead of to starboard, as would be the case if the vessel had headway.

It sometimes happens, when one is anchored in a crowded narrow place with a strong tide running and but a light breeze blowing, that one cannot get under way in the ordinary manner without running a great risk of drifting foul of vessels anchored close astern. The following method (which is called dredging) can then be employed with advantage, more especially if the bottom be of mud. The cable is hove short. One hand goes forward and keeps the vessel dragging slowly astern by taking chain in until the anchor is almost off the ground, while he stands by ready to give her back a little chain should she begin to drag too fast. The tide, running under the vessel at a faster rate than she is dragging, gives steerage way and enables the helmsman to steer his craft so as to avoid the anchored vessels, as he drifts down-stream stern on. As soon as the vessel gets into more open water, the anchor is got up and the sails are hoisted.

A similar plan is that employed by the Norfolk wherrymen when dropping down the narrow rapid river at Yarmouth with their sails furled. They trail a long chain (having no anchor on it) from their bows, over the muddy bottom, thus retarding their progress and providing the steerage way needed to keep them clear of obstacles and shoot the bridges.

A vessel moored to a buoy is easier to get under way than one lying at anchor, as she is under more complete control, and there is no dragging of the anchor to be feared. One can wait till she is canted in the right direction before slipping from the moorings; and by bringing the mooring-rope to one side or other of the vessel, one can ensure her casting off on the required tack. Thus if one wishes to cast off on the port tack, the mooring-rope is brought to the port-side and is made fast close to the main rigging; this turns the vessel's head to starboard. The sails are then hoisted; it takes a second to slip the moorings, and away the vessel shoots with all her sails full.

Until the anchor is well out of the water do not get much way on the vessel, but heave to, if you have plenty of sea-room; for otherwise the anchor may be driven back by the pressure of the water, and get foul of the stem or bobstay.

Having got the vessel under way, I will now describe some of the principal manoeuvres which have to be executed in the course of a sail. We will suppose that all plain canvas has been set, and that the vessel is sailing full and bye – that is, as near the wind as she can go, while yet keeping her sails full. Nothing is gained by jamming a boat too close to the wind, with her sails all on the shake; for though she may be pointing more directly towards her destination, her speed will be greatly diminished, especially if there is any sea on.

To sail a vessel on a wind so as to get the most out of her is an art not to be acquired without much patient practice and observation. At first, the tyro will find it a wearisome business to take his trick at the tiller when a vessel is close-hauled. He will ever be anxiously on the watch lest he bear away or luff up too much; and yet, despite all his care, he will be disgusted to find that at one moment all his sails are flapping and the vessel loses her way, and that at the next moment he has brought the wind almost abeam and is sailing away to leeward. He has a tendency to push his helm hard up and hard down alternately, thus correcting one error with such violence that he at once falls into the opposite error.

Steering becomes in time a second instinct, and cannot be taught in books; but the following hints may prove useful to the novice. When steering, stand or sit on the weather-side of the deck. The angle at which the burgee at the masthead is blowing out will show you whether you are too much off the wind when sailing close-hauled. If you are sailing too near the wind the shaking of the sail will warn you. When you see the luff of the jib and mainsail just lifting slightly, you are sailing as near the wind as you should be. The novice therefore, when steering full and bye, should always have his eyes on the sails and the burgee. But when practice has made him an experienced helmsman he will need no such guides; the feel of the tiller will then tell him whether he is steering rightly, and with a sensitive hand he will hold the helm at exactly the right angle to keep her on her course, moving it but very slightly – almost imperceptibly – now and again, instead of ever passing it backwards and forwards from hard up to hard down, as he used to do in the early days of his novitiate.

The best of all guides is the feel of the wind on one's face, which indicates whether one is steering full and bye or yawing about. It is astonishing with what nicety a sailor can distinguish the direction of even a very light wind in this way. On a dark night when he is steering full and bye, and not by compass, this is the only possible guide to the helmsman; so, too, if the vessel is running before the wind, he can feel by the chill on his neck or ear if he is sailing by the lee or luffing up.

When sailing full and bye it is important that the sails should be properly trimmed; they should not be sheeted so flat that the vessel becomes sluggish, and they must all be sheeted as nearly as possible at the right angle, so that one sail will not lift long before the other when the vessel comes up into the wind. It is a common fault to flatten in the jib-sheet too much, by which the sail's effect is wasted, and it tends more to drive the vessel to leeward than to propel her. If the mainsail is seen to lift before the jib, slacken up the jib-sheet a bit.

TO TACK

When the wind is so much ahead that one cannot steer directly for one's destination, even when close-hauled, the vessel has to be tacked. The theory of tacking has been dealt with in a previous chapter; the practice will now be explained.

If two or more hands are available for the operation, the following is the procedure: the man at the helm selects his opportunity, and if it be heavy weather he awaits a smooth; for a vessel is liable to miss stays if struck by a sea before she has come up into the wind; then, having decided to put the vessel about, he sings out 'ready about' when the hands will stand by ready to handle the sheet. If necessary, he should keep the vessel a point or so more off the wind for a short time, before he gives the next order, so as to get plenty of way on her. The next order will be 'helm's a-lee', and as he gives it he puts the tiller down to leeward gently, and only about half-way over, thus allowing the vessel to shoot well ahead while in stays. When she is in the wind's eye he gives her some more helm to help her pay off on the other tack.

In the meanwhile, the hands at the sheets have been doing their duty. As the vessel comes up into the wind they slack up the jib and fore-sheets; and when the vessel has passed the head-to-wind position, they haul the sheets in on the other side, which now becomes the lee-side; but they must not do this too soon, else the head sails will act as back sails, prevent the vessel from paying off, and cause her to miss stays. The jib-sheet, for example, should not be hauled over until the jib has blown clear of the fore-stay; but it should then be got in and belayed very smartly, before the vessel is filling on the other tack, else the strain will be so great that it will be difficult to get it in at all. If the vessel is sluggish in stays, or if there be a lumpy sea, the fore-sheet should not be let go with the jib-sheet, but it should be left belayed until the vessel fills on the other tack. The foresail, thus taken aback, helps the vessel's head to pay off; but the vessel's way is of course stopped to some extent by this, and the foresail must not be kept to windward a moment longer than is necessary. In order to go about smartly it is well to flatten in the main-sheet until the vessel is in the wind's eye, and then to slack it off again as her head pays off on the other tack.

If one is sailing single-handed, the mainsail must be left to take care of itself during the process of tacking; the jib must be allowed to pass over and its sheet must be belayed on the new tack before the fore-sheets are touched.

If, in consequence of the helm having been put down too fast, or the head-sheets having been hauled in too soon, the vessel misses stays, she is left 'in irons,' that is, she lies helplessly head to wind, refusing to fill on either tack, her sails all shaking, her head-way lost, and she soon begins to gather stern-way. In order to get her under way again (say, on the port tack) haul the head-sheets to windward, that is, to the port-side, and slack off the main-sheet. This will cause her head to pay off to starboard, then the sails can be trimmed and she will go ahead again. So long as she has stern-way, remember that the action of the rudder is reversed, that is, the tiller must be put over to starboard in order to pay the vessel's head off to starboard.

TO RUN BEFORE THE WIND

When a vessel is running before the wind all sheets are eased off, the main-sheet more so than the others, so that the mainsail is almost squared to the wind. The runners, preventer backstays, and boom topping-lifts are belayed on the weather-side and slacked off on the lee-side.

When running, do not steer a vessel so that she is 'by the lee', unless it be necessary to do so in order to avoid collision with another vessel, or for some other such good reason. A vessel is by the lee when she bears away so much that the wind comes from the quarter over which the boom is squared. She is then very near the point which would bring the wind to the back of the sails and cause a jibe. A jibe thus brought about is always more or less dangerous, and may even capsize a vessel. Serious damage is likely to attend an accidental jibe if it is blowing hard; the boom swinging over with great violence from one quarter to the other will carry all before it on its way – runners, preventer backstays, and topmast; and it will probably be sprung by the sudden jerk with which it is brought up by the main-sheet. The head-sails always give timely warning that one is sailing by the lee; for the wind gets behind them and bellies them out from the other side before the mainsail is in any danger of jibing.

JIBING

When it becomes necessary to jibe a vessel, proper precautions have to be taken. Before preparing for a jibe, steer so that the wind is not quite aft, but on the quarter opposite to that over which the boom is squared. Haul in on the main-sheet till the boom is half-way in. Then put the helm slowly up to bring the vessel round, and continue hauling on the main-sheet till the boom is amidships. Before the vessel is by the lee, slack off the weather-runners (and weather-preventing backstays, if these be standing) and set taut the lee-runners, which will become the weather-runners when the jibe has been effected. As the wind strikes the mainsail on the opposite side, slack off the main-sheet so as to break the jerk and allow the boom to pass over easily to the other quarter. A vessel is apt to run up into the wind as she jibes, so the helm must be put up to meet her. Then sheet the headsails on what has now become the lee side.

If the wind is strong it is well to scandalise the mainsail – trice up the main tack and lower the peak – before jibing.

When running before a heavy sea a vessel is apt to yaw about a good deal, and therefore exceptional care must be taken to avoid an accidental jibe. The prudent plan under these circumstances is not to steer dead before the wind, but to sail for some distance with the wind on one quarter, and then to jibe and sail with the wind on the other quarter.

A vessel is said to be hove-to when she is made to remain stationary, by getting some of her head sails aback. To heave a cutter to, luff her up till she is close-hauled, haul the fore-sheet to windward, and haul on the jibsheet until the corner of the jib is over the forestay. If the main-sheet is now trimmed properly – experiment will quickly show how much it should be flattened in – the headsails and the mainsail will balance each other, the former causing the vessel's head to pay off, the latter driving her up into the wind, with the result that the vessel will remain floating head to wind, making no headway, and the tiller can be lashed amidships.

When sailing single-handed, provided you have sufficient sea room, heave the vessel to before undertaking to reef, shift jibs, etc. You can then leave the tiller and do the work at your leisure, while the vessel takes care of herself.

When hove-to under snug canvas, even a small fore-and-after will often ride quite comfortably and safely through very heavy weather. To ride out a gale a cutter is generally hove-to under trysail and storm-jib, the foresail being stowed. To get under way when hove-to, hoist the foresail if it is down, slack up the main-sheet, and when the vessel has paid well off trim the sheets.

When shifting sails and reefing, care must be taken to preserve the balance between the head and the after-sails, so that the vessel remains in good sailing trim, having a decided tendency to come up into the wind, while not yet carrying excessive weather helm. Thus if a large jib be changed for a small one, and the foresail be reefed, while the mainsail is left standing, the vessel will gripe and the tiller will have to be put hard down to keep her off the wind, the rudder being at such an angle as to seriously retard the vessel's speed. On the other hand, if the mainsail be reefed while the whole foresail and the big jib are left on her, the vessel will probably carry a lee helm, which, as has already been explained, no yacht should under any circumstances be allowed to do; among other reasons, because, when in that dangerous trim, she will be pinned down and possibly be capsized by a squall instead of luffing up into it.

A whole mainsail and a whole foresail can be carried after the first jib has been exchanged for the second, without materially increasing a vessel's weather-helm; but on most yachts whenever the foresail is reefed the mainsail should be reefed also. Thus in a fresh breeze a cutter will generally be seen sailing under single-reefed mainsail, single-reefed foresail, and third jib. In a heavy gale it is usual to stow the foresail, and to sail under trysail and storm-jib.

When setting a smaller jib reef the bowsprit, for a small jib hauled half way along a bowsprit strains the spar, which at that point is not supported by the shrouds and bobstay; moreover a vessel is greatly relieved by getting the weight of the bowsprit more inboard.

That a vessel should be in good trim is of especial importance when she is beating to windward against a heavy sea. It is essential then that her canvas should not only be well-balanced, but that it should be sufficiently reduced, so that she can be sailed ramping full, and be ever kept well under control; whereas if too much sail is carried she will have to be luffed up into every strong puff, when the seas will quickly deaden her way, and she will plunge and tumble about uneasily in the hollows between the waves, and probably get in irons. When an exceptionally big sea is seen rolling up, the vessel must be luffed up into it, so as to meet it end on, but as soon as it has passed one must bear away again and fill the sails. Unless one has been sailing full and keeping good way on her, one cannot perform this manoeuvre properly, and with an overcanvassed craft that has to be luffed up to puffs of wind as well as to seas, one will progress but slowly, and will make very bad weather of it.

When running before a heavy sea, the vessel, especially if she be a short beamy one, will exhibit a tendency to yaw about, and will require most careful steering. Now is the occasion for the helmsman to show his skill. With the novice at the helm the vessel will steer in the wildest fashion, now shooting up into the wind, now bearing right away till there is danger of a jibe, and the tiller will be kept ever hard at it travelling backwards and forwards from one quarter to the other. But the experienced man will keep his helm steady, and the vessel's yawing will be slight; for the art of steering does not consist of violently forcing the tiller up and down to correct a vessel's deviation from her course after it has occurred, but in anticipating her movements with a gentle pressure of the tiller before she begins to fall off or come up. The helmsman feels that he is between Scylla and Charybdis when running before a heavy sea, and he needs all his nerve. For on the one hand he has to avoid an accidental jibe, and on the other hand, whenever a dangerously big and steep sea rolls up, he must so steer that the vessel is dead before it; for if it strikes her on the weather quarter it may cause her to broach to, that is, fly up into the wind till she is broadside on to the sea, a most dangerous position, in which she is in great risk of being swamped or rolled over by the next big wave.

Always carry a jib when running before the wind, it will help to pay the vessel off if she attempts to broach to. One can carry more canvas when before the wind than when sailing close-hauled: but if too much sail is carried the vessel will roll heavily. Do not crack on canvas under the impression that it will enable you to run away from the following seas and so avoid the risk of being pooped. No vessel can run as fast as that.

A cruising yacht should carry a storm squaresail made to hoist under the forestay, so as to be high enough to catch the wind when the vessel is in the trough of the sea. Under such a sail a yacht will run before a heavy sea with much diminished chance of broaching to or jibing. A cutter running before a strong wind will not roll nearly so heavily and can be steered with far greater ease if a small spinnaker be set on the other side to balance the mainsail. I have often set such a spinnaker by the side of a reefed mainsail when cruising in the South Atlantic, with great advantage: and whenever I had to run before a strong wind on my little three-tonner during her cruise on the almost always choppy Baltic I invariably had my mainsail boomed out on one side and a small boat's standing-lug on the other side.

As soon as the latter sail was hoisted there was a remarkable gain both in speed and comfort.

If one runs too long before a gale, the sea may get so high that it becomes exceedingly dangerous, if not impossible, to bring the vessel up in the wind and heave her to. Always heave-to in good time, if you have plenty of sea room and no port to run for. Wait for the smooth, which generally follows two or three exceptionally high waves, before bringing the vessel to: for the perilous moment will be when she is being brought broadside on to the sea. It is astonishing with what safety and comfort a fore-and-after will ride out a gale, rising easily to every steep wave, and taking but little water on board.

Run too long and you will have an anxious time of it as I had once off the River Plate on my yawl the *Falcon*. A gale had sprung up, and as it was favourable for us, bound as we were for Bahia, I imprudently determined to make use of it instead of heaving to, and ran before it under trysail and storm jib. But it proved to be more than an ordinary gale and developed into a three-day Pampero – the hurricane wind of those latitudes. Very shortly so high a sea was running that I did not dare attempt to heave her to; so on we scudded for three days and nights, steering for our lives, and having a very bad time of it. On the second day we had a very narrow escape, for we were pooped by a gigantic wave and were in great danger of foundering. The following passage from my narrative of that cruise may serve as a warning to those who would run on when they had much better heave-to.

It is generally observed that during a prolonged gale two or four rollers, far higher than any others, occur at long intervals, say of twelve hours, and it is no doubt, as a rule, one of such exceptionally lofty and breaking seas that overwhelms a vessel and causes her to founder. At four o'clock on this particular afternoon two such billows came right astern. I was steering at the time, and looking over my shoulder I perceived a huge wave of green water, with an ugly, over-curling, breaking crest, rapidly overtaking us. It seemed that it must of a certainty fall on us, and that it was quite impossible for the *Falcon* to rise to such a steep wall of water; that she would be rolled over and overby it certainly seemed probable to me at that moment. I only took a second's glance, jammed myself firmly inside the tiller rope, and steered so that the wave should strike us dead aft. Suddenly up went our stern with a jerk that jumped me off my feet, a few bucketfuls of water tumbled on board; then up flew our bow till our deck was at an angle of 45 degrees. The roller had passed us; it had struck us so true that we remained on an even keel without the slightest list to port or starboard. But the peril was far from over yet; another equally lofty roller followed close; and between the two was a valley so narrow and steep that it was impossible that the *Falcon* after her descent could raise her stern in time to meet this second wall of water. After a glance over my shoulder, which sufficed me to take in the danger of the situation, I turned my back on the roller again, and kept the vessel dead before it. We slid down the slope of the liquid valley, then our stern commenced to rise a little as the foot of the second wave reached us, and then there was a crash and a sudden darkness, and I felt a mass of water rush right over my head. 'It is all up with us,' I thought – that is, if I thought at all, for all this had occupied but a few seconds; I think, however, all on board imagined that we had foundered; doubtlessly to any one looking from above, the masts of the vessel would at that moment alone have been visible, the whole hull must have been submerged. But the *Falcon* was strong, the mass of water had not broken through her decks: just as she had met the first wave she met this, not in the least on one quarter or the other, so we escaped broaching-to, a probable occurrence in the presence of such monster waves, and one that would of course have ensured our loss. In another second, as I opened my eyes after the stunning effect of the deluge of water, I saw the bulwarks rise above the sea, then the little vessel gave herself a sort of shake of relief and the water soon poured out through her scuppers, this being facilitated by the comparatively calm sea that always succeeds to exceptionally high waves. The cook, I observed, had held on tightly, and had not been washed overboard. Then the companion-hatch slid back and my two other Italian hands came up, with faces pallid; when they heard the shock of the mass of water on deck, they fancied that they distinctly felt the vessel going down, and were sure she was foundering. They said that after the first shock it suddenly became quite dark in the cabin and all was silent, while little jets of water were spurting in, as if under great pressure, through every little leak between the planks of the deck above them.

When sailing with the wind abeam, the sheets are eased off so that the sails just fill and draw well, without shaking at the luff. If a steep sea rolls up, luff up to it a bit, so as to shoulder it – that is, take it on the weather bow and not broadside on. Do not carry too much canvas when sailing with the wind abeam.

If a really heavy sea is running do not venture to sail with the wind abeam; sail close-hauled or run for it according to circumstances – or do each in turn if by that course you can best reach your destination.

If sailing with the sea on the quarter, bear away before the more dangerous seas, so as not to run the risk of broaching-to.

To come to an anchorage, or to pick up moorings in a crowded roadstead is a matter requiring great skill and judgment; and the novice will probably find this the most difficult to master of all the manoeuvres he has to execute while sailing his yacht.

Before getting to your anchorage haul up from below and range on deck a length of cable equal to, or slightly greater than, the depth of the water in which you intend to let go your anchor. Steer to windward of the spot where you wish to bring up. When near it lower the head sails, flatten in the main sheet, and bring the vessel up into the wind's eye, sharply, or with a long sweep, according to the circumstances. When she has lost all her way and begins to drop astern, let go the anchor. The length of the sweep one should make when coming up depends on the set and strength of the tide, the qualities of the vessel (a deep boat will shoot much further than a shallow one before losing her way), and so forth; and practice only can enable the novice to calculate with nicety what should be done. If wind and tide are in the same direction one must of course lower the headsails and luff up into the wind sooner than if the wind and tide are opposed.

If the wind and tide are opposed, the easiest and safest method of coming to one's anchorage is to run dead before the wind up to it instead of luffing. Reduce the canvas gradually according to the strength of the wind, until the vessel remains stationary over the right spot, the wind and tide just counteracting each other; then let go. To give an example of this manoeuvre, let us suppose that the mainsail has been lowered and that the vessel is still making good way under foresail and jib. The jib is next lowered, when the vessel is found to be progressing very slowly. As soon as she has reached her anchorage the foresail is hauled down, the tide at once gets the mastery and brings the vessel to a standstill, and she begins to go astern; then the anchor is let go.

If, instead of coming to an anchor, moorings have to be picked up, still greater accuracy must be employed in making one's calculations and executing the manoeuvre, else the moorings may be missed altogether. A hand must be stationed in the bows with a boathook, ready to hook up the mooring-buoy as soon as he can reach it, and to belay the mooring rope smartly. To miss one's moorings by shooting past them or short of them in a crowded anchorage may place one in an awkward position; for the vessel will then drift helplessly away, and is likely to fall foul of neighbouring craft before she can be got under control. If you fail to pick up your moorings after luffing up to them under the mainsail, hoist the foresail smartly and ease off the main-sheet so as to get the vessel under control as quickly as possible. But when tide meets wind, moorings can be picked up, without any risk, in the manner described above, by running up to them instead of luffing. The buoy is then easily secured; and even if the hand with the boathook bungle the business, the foresail can be hoisted in a moment and the vessel gathers way again. When approaching one's moorings it is prudent to have a kedge or small anchor ready to let go in case of accidents.

When anchoring, do not pay chain out too fast, as it will fall on the top of the anchor, and possibly take a turn round the fluke, in which case the anchor will drag out of the ground as soon as a strain is put upon it. Having let the chain which has been ranged on deck run out, wait till the vessel goes astern and the chain tautens before giving her more; then do so gradually until she has enough to hold her – about three times the depth of the water suffices as a rule; but more will be required if the holding ground is bad or if it is blowing hard.

Having come to an anchor or picked up your moorings, lower the main-boom on its crutch and stow the sails neatly. Put their coats on the mainsail and foresail, if these sails are dry; if they are damp furl them loosely and hoist and dry them as soon as you have a chance. On no account put the sail coats on wet sails, as to do this will infallibly produce mildew. Slack off the clew of the mainsail before stowing it, for by keeping the clew constantly hauled out taut along the boom (a common fault), you will pull the foot of the sail all out of shape. Belay all halyards, sheets, backstays, etc., neatly, but not too taut if they are dry; remember that a shower of rain will cause all your hemp rope to shrink considerably, and then an over-taut preventer backstay, for example, may put such a strain upon the topmast as to break it. Slack up the bobstay tackle and haul the bobstay up to the stem, so that it may be clear of the chain.

If it be blowing hard, or the holding ground be your single anchor will hold the vessel, moor her, that is, ride to two anchors placed at some distance apart, so that the two cables form an angle. To moor, let go on one anchor and veer out twice as much cable as you intend to ride by. When the cable is taut let go the second anchor. Heave in on the first cable and veer out the second until the same length of cable is out on both anchors. It is sometimes more convenient to take the second anchor out in a boat to the place where it has to be let go.

To unmoor, veer out chain to one anchor while getting the other anchor up. Then weigh the second anchor.

When lying at anchor in windless weather, the vessel is apt to float right over her anchor at slack water, just before the turn of the tide. The cable is then likely to take a turn round the upper fluke of the anchor, so that, when a strain is put upon it, it will pull the other fluke out of the ground and so cause the anchor to drag. To obviate this heave the cable short at slack water and let it go again when the vessel swings to the tide.

If one is anchored on rocky ground the anchor is apt to get foul, and may have to be abandoned unless one has adopted one of the two following methods for insuring its recovery. Before letting go the anchor, fasten the end of a small line to the crown of it, and buoy the other end. If the anchor has got hold of a rock and refuses to come up when the cable is hauled upon, it can be liberated by hauling on the tripping line.

If the anchorage is to be but a temporary one, the same end can be attained by bending the cable on to the crown of the anchor, instead of to the shackle or ring, and by stopping the cable along the shank or to the shackle with twine, as shown in Fig. 65 (p. 137). If the anchor is foul the stopping will break when the cable is hauled upon, and the anchor, being then pulled crown first, will get free. Remember that there is always a chance, when this method is employed, of the stopping accidently breaking while the vessel lies at anchor; in which case the anchor will of course drag. This plan therefore will not do if you wish to turn in for the night and sleep in security.

The terms employed in describing the different parts of an anchor will be understood by referring to Fig. 65 – *a a* is the *shank; b b* are the *arms* terminating in the barbed *flukes; c c d* is the *stock*, which is at right angles to the arms; *e* is the *crown*.

In heavy weather a vessel is greatly relieved by lowering the mainsail and hoisting the trysail in its place. The mainsail must be well stowed, and the boom must be securely lashed amidships. The throat and peak halyards must be taken off the main gaff to be hooked on to the trysail gaff. The topping lifts must be unhooked and be fastened in the main rigging – so too must be the peak-halyards if the trysail is jib-headed and is therefore hoisted with the throat halyards only.

If a small vessel be overtaken by such heavy weather, when she is on the open sea, that she is in danger, even when hove-to under her storm canvas, a drogue or floating anchor can be put out, a contrivance which has enabled even small open boats to ride out the heaviest gales with safety. A drogue generally consists of a framework of iron or wood, with strong canvas stretched across it, so as to offer great resistance to the water when dragged through it broadside on. I carried a drogue with me on the *Falcon* during her South Atlantic cruise, but never had occasion to use it save in the shark-infested anchorage off the desert island of Trinidade, where I hung it overboard each morning and had my bath in it, without risk of being snapped up by one of the voracious monsters ever on the watch around us. This drogue (Fig. 66, p. 137), was thus fashioned: a conical bag of stout canvas, about five feet in diameter, was bent on to an iron ring, which was attached to the hawser by a bridle; a tripping line of light rope was also fastened to the pointed end of the drogue, by means of which it could be capsized and relieved of the pressure of the water before being hauled on board.

A vessel riding to her drogue with some forty fathoms of hawser out (grass rope which floats on the water is perhaps the best), as she drags astern is ever kept head to wind and sea, and cannot well pay off or get broadside on to the waves as they roll by her. If no drogue is carried on board, a very effective one can be extemporised by bending one side of a small jib or other sail to a spar and riding to that (Fig. 67, p. 137). The hawser must be attached to the middle of a rope about twice the length of the spar, the rope being made fast at either end to the extremities of the spar, thus forming a span, and keeping the spar broadside on to the seas. A bit of ballast should be attached to the lower corner of the sail in order to sink it and keep it in a vertical position, so that it may offer the greatest resistance to the water. The spar to some extent serves as a breakwater as well as a floating anchor, and prevents the seas from breaking near the vessel.

When riding to a drogue it will be well, unless the gale be very heavy, to have a reefed mizzen set if the vessel be a yawl, and a reefed trysail if she be a cutter; in either case the sail must be sheeted amidships.

If running for a bar harbour with the wind on shore and the sea breaking heavily on the bar, a small drogue can be towed astern with great advantage, as it will prevent the sea from driving the vessel's stern round and broaching her to.

A drogue which appears to be very well suited for small craft is now manufactured by R. C. Lacey, 75 Summerly Street. A copper oil distributor can be attached at pleasure.

The extraordinary effect of pouring oil upon the troubled waters has been fully demonstrated by a series of experiments that have been recently conducted in stormy weather at the entrance of some of our bar harbours; and even large vessels have been saved from destruction by the use of a few gallons of oil. It needs but very little oil to form a coat over a large expanse of water; and where the oil is the sea will roll smoothly, the waves will either break at the weather edge of the oil or pass harmlessly across it in gentle undulations. When a vessel is hove-to, the oil bag is hung over the weather bow and the oil, oozing out slowly, leaves a smooth space to windward. If the drogue is out, an oil bag can be secured to that. When running before the wind an oil bag is hung over the stern or quarter.

Some years ago a North Sea fisherman, with whom I was cruising on the Doggerbank, gave me his experience of the use of oil in a gale. It was on the edge of the Dogger, in five fathom soundings where the seas break heavily. The fleet was running before the wind, when he and some other skippers bethought them to try the effect of oil. The result was magical, and their vessels at once began to make good weather of it. But he told me that some other vessels following them had to pass through seas breaking heavily on the weather edge of the oily expanse, and had a very uncomfortable time of it. In his opinion when the seas do break thus on approaching the oil, they do so in a more dangerous fashion than if no oil was there; which seems likely enough. To judge from all the evidence that has been collected on the subject, there can be little doubt that, given plenty of sea room, even quite a small yacht – provided of course that she be sound, not over sparred, and of the right build – can ride out an Atlantic gale in safety by employing drogue and oil bag; and no one should attempt a long cruise on broad seas with such a vessel without carrying these.

8

Open Boat Sailing

In many respects the management of the open boat under canvas differs considerably from that of the decked yacht. An open boat is more easily capsized and swamped; her movements are more sudden; every manoeuvre has to be performed with greater rapidity than on the larger craft. He who attempts to sail her as he would a decked and deep-keeled yacht is pretty certain to come to grief sooner or later. The open boat sailor must never forget what a tricky and dangerous craft he has under him, and must never relax his care and watchfulness.

It is not only because a boat is open, and would therefore fill if she were sailed gunwhale under like a yacht, that she is more dangerous than the latter. Being of shallow draught, with no ballast outside, she has little stability, and once blown over beyond a certain angle cannot recover herself and must capsize. Thus if you carry too much canvas in a choppy sea a little lop that a yacht would pay no attention to may lift up the side of the open boat till she attains the danger angle, when the wind pressing on the sail will complete the mischief, and the next moment she will be bottom up. It has been pointed out in a previous chapter that ballast lying in the bottom of a shallow boat does not materially increase her stability, whereas the recovering power of a deep vessel is greater the more she heels over, so that she is practically un-capsizable.

An open boat should carry no more ballast than is absolutely necessary, and what there is should be kept amidships, so that both bow and stem are buoyant and rise successively to the passing seas. Except when an open boat is being raced by an experienced crew, it is highly imprudent to stiffen her by shifting ballast to windward or by making her passengers sit on the weather gunwhale; as a sudden lull or change in the direction of the wind, or the roll caused by a passing beam sea may result in her suddenly capsizing to windward. But under certain circumstances it may be prudent to shift ballast fore or aft. Thus, if one is compelled to run before a dangerously heavy sea, the tendency to broach-to can be diminished by moving some of the ballast aft; on the other hand, when one is pulling against the sea it is often advisable to move the ballast forward, for this gives the boat a better grip of the water, and renders her less likely to be knocked off her course by a wave.

Though battens should be fastened to the floor of an open boat to prevent the ballast from slipping to leeward in a squall, the ballast, unless it consists of water-tanks, should not be so secured that it cannot fall overboard if the boat capsizes. The boat relieved of her ballast will float instead of sinking, and can be recovered; moreover, the crew are enabled to cling to her until succour arrives. But even if the ballast be not secured, it will often remain in the swamped boat and drag her down. It is for this reason that water – as has been explained in Chapter 4 – is the only form of ballast for an open boat that will render her absolutely unsinkable.

Whereas in smooth water, a yacht, if not overcanvassed, can keep steadily on her course regardless of the squalls, save that she leans gracefully to them and increases her speed, the open boat has frequently to be luffed up into the stronger puffs, or her sheets have to be eased off. If the boat have but a single sail, ease off the sheet smartly when luffing to a heavy squall. If she carry a foresail, ease off the foresheet first, and ease off the mainsheet only if the squall be of exceptional violence. With a main and mizzen-rigged boat the mizzen-sheet, as a rule, should not be let go in a squall. With a wind of given strength much less canvas should be carried in rough than in smooth water. If there is much sea sail the boat under snug canvas, which she can carry without danger in the squalls; for if a steep comber comes down on you and you have to luff up to it just at the moment that a heavy gust compels you to let go your sheets, you will lose all control over the boat; her way will be lost, and she may be rolled over by the next wave. To sail safely across rough water, you should keep your eyes on the seas alone and steer so as best to ride over them, regardless of the squalls, having your sails ramping full; this can only be done by reducing your canvas sufficiently.

It is a good rule, when sailing a small boat, not to belay the sheets. Take a turn with the sheet round the after-thwart, or a pin or cleat, and hold the fall in the hand; the sheet can then be let go in a moment. If two men are sailing the boat, the one steering can tend the main-sheet, while the other looks to the fore-sheet. Patent cleats have been invented for open boats, which automatically release the sheets so soon as the wind pressure on the sails and the consequent strain on the sheets exceed a certain limit and heel the boat towards the danger angle. But, if one must belay one's sheet, perhaps the safest and simplest method is the old-fashioned one represented in Fig. 68 (p.138). On either quarter of the boat an iron pin is fitted under the gunwale, allowing space for the sheet to pass between it and the boat's planking. The sheet is taken round the pin and a bight is passed under the standing part of the sheet, which jams it so long as there is a strain upon the sheet. A pull upon the fall, which must be kept close to the hand, withdraws the bight and at once releases the sheet.

The halyards also must be so belayed that they can be quickly let go; therefore a half-hitch should not be taken on the top of the turns on the cleat. The halyards should always be properly coiled and capsized, ready to run out without risk of getting foul. If the sheet and halyard falls are lying about untidily in the bottom of the boat they will tie themselves into knots, and when let go will jam in the blocks and comb-cleats or get entangled with the feet of the crew – a frequent cause of capsizing and of loss of life even among good swimmers. Many sailing-boats and canoes appear to me to be supplied with a superfluity of ropes. Rapidity and ease in performing the manoeuvres may be gained by this, but the risks of the cordage getting entangled and jamming is much increased. In the eyes of some amateur sailors, to have as much rigging in a twelve-foot dinghy as would be carried on a twelve-ton yacht makes a brave show; but, as a matter of fact, not a single rope that can be dispensed with should be allowed in the open boat.

If a boat is intended for single-handed sailing it is well to have the halyards leading aft, so that one need not leave the tiller and go forward to lower the sail. The halyards, in this case, are led through blocks at the foot of the mast. These blocks should not be attached to the mast itself, but to the thwart through which the mast is stepped.

It cannot be too much insisted upon that an open boat must not be treated as if she were a yacht. For example, one would never attempt to climb the mast in order to reeve a halyard or for any other purpose, more especially when the boat is under way. The sail should be lowered, and the mast should be unstepped. When sailing an open boat the helmsman sits on the weather-side; but great risk is incurred by allowing the other hands – more especially if they are inexperienced – to do so. As a rule, therefore, passengers should be made to sit in the centre of the boat, and if there be much sea the bottom of the boat is the best place for them.

One should always carry a lifebuoy when sailing a small boat. To do so on boats engaged in racing is made compulsory by the rules of the upper Thames sailing clubs.

When a squall strikes a boat that has plenty of way on her, the increased wind pressure in her sails is chiefly exerted in propelling her faster through the water; but if the boat is stationary, nearly the whole force of the wind is at first spent in heeling her over, and she may capsize unless she gathers way quickly. Consequently, when sailing under the lee of a vessel, one should be ready to let go the sheets in a moment. For the boat will probably have the wind taken out of her sails when she is passing the vessel; and the moment she has got clear of it, her steerage-way almost lost, the wind will suddenly give her a knock-down blow while she is in this helpless condition; so that, unless one is ready to slack up sheets promptly, over the boat will go. Sail and mast should be lowered before coming alongside a vessel to board her.

When running before the wind in rough water it is advisable not to bring the wind directly aft, as the boat's yawing may cause an accidental jibe. It is better to sail for some distance with the wind on one quarter, then to jibe and sail with the wind on the other quarter.

A beam sea is of course the most dangerous. If compelled to sail with the sea abeam, bear away before the bigger seas. If the sea is very heavy it is best not to attempt to sail with the wind abeam. One can fetch one's destination by running before wind and sea for awhile, and then luffing up in a smooth and sailing close-hauled, and so on alternately.

Jibe with great care, hauling the boom inboard as you put the helm up. Remember that when the boom swings over, the force of the jibe will in a moment drive the boat up into the wind's eye unless you meet, or rather anticipate, this tendency with your helm.

A boat carrying a single sail naturally has its mast stepped well forward; consequently, if such a boat is in the wind's eye, in irons, and gathering stern-way, she can be made to pay off again by holding the boom over to windward and the tiller to leeward. When the boat has paid off sufficiently, she will rapidly gather way again if the sheet is trimmed to leeward and the sail is allowed to draw.

It is often advisable, when running before a heavy sea, to unship the rudder and to steer with an oar. The open-boat sailor, by the way, should never leave his moorings without having his oars on board. It often happens that the novice is guilty of this omission, being too proud of his little craft to bear in mind that she is not a large yacht propelled by sails alone.

Moveover, when shipping the oar-crutches, one must not forget to secure them to the gunwale with the lanyards which are attached to the ends of crutches for this purpose. If a crutch falls overboard at a critical moment disaster may ensue. If a crutch is lost and there is no spare one at hand, a rope grommet, or even a piece of cord fastened in a loop to the rowlocks, will serve the purpose temporarily, and enable one to employ the oars as before.

One oar, which should not be too long or heavy, should lie always within easy reach of the man sailing single-handed. With this he can pull the boat round if she misses stays, and steer her if the rudder carries away, or when running before a heavy sea. It is well to have a hollow cut into the transom to hold the oar, so that one can scull over the stern, a convenient method of propelling a boat when in a crowded harbour.

In case a boat is driven out to sea in heavy weather, a deep-sea or floating anchor should be made with the spars, in the way described in Chapter 7. Small open boats have frequently ridden out Atlantic gales with safety in this fashion.

Every one who goes open-boat sailing on an exposed coast should study the rules published by the National Lifeboat Institution with regard to the management of open boats in rough water, and the beaching of them through a surf. The following is a summary of these rules:

I.   As a general rule speed must be given to a boat rowing seaward against a heavy surf; for otherwise a sea may carry her back with it, turning her broadside on, or end-up, and so capsizing her. She should be given such way as to enable her to pass through the crest of the sea and leave it as soon as possible behind her.

II.   A boat running before a broken sea to the shore offers no resistance to it and is carried before it, thus running great danger of capsizing, by broaching to, or by running her bows under water. Her way should therefore be stopped on the approach of each dangerous sea that overtakes her, and this is effected in either of the three following ways: – 1. By turning the boat's head to the sea before entering the broken water, and then backing in stern foremost, pulling a few strokes ahead to meet each heavy sea, and then again backing astern. 2. If rowing to shore with the stern to seaward, by backing the oars on the approach of a heavy sea, and rowing ahead again as soon as it has passed the bow of the boat. This is the best method if the boat is a long one with a pointed stern like a whale-boat. 3. If rowed in bow foremost, by towing astern a pig of ballast or large stone, or a drogue, so as to hold the boat's stern back.

When running for the shore through a heavy sea a head-sail only should be used, and this should be reefed if it is large. It is usually safer to lower masts and sails and work the boat to shore with oars alone.

Where a shore is flat the water breaks far out, the more dangerous breakers being in comparatively deep water; and as one nears the land the danger lessens, the force of the sea gradually expending itself. Consequently a boat, whether she be brought in stern or bow first, is kept straight before the sea until she grounds, when the crew jump out and haul her up the beach.

But if the shore be steep, the sea does not break until it falls upon the beach, and one can approach close to before incurring any danger. To beach a boat on a steep shore she is run straight in, and at the last moment her bow is turned broadside on to the beach. She should then be hauled up as quickly as possible out of reach of the breakers.

On some coasts washed by wide oceans the sea breaks heavily on the beach even in the calmest weather. If the surf be dangerous, one can wait just outside until a comparative smooth follows a succession of big waves, and then pull in at full speed. One can see this very cleverly done by the boatmen of Madeira when the steep green rollers thunder on its shingle beach.

If a surf is breaking on a steep rocky shore and it is necessary to embark or to disembark passengers, this can be done without beaching the boat and thereby incurring the risk of staving her in. The anchor is let go just outside the surf, and the boat is backed in towards the shore with the oars, while a hand in the bows pays out the cable slowly, thus keeping the boat end on to the sea. When the boat's stern is near enough to the shore to allow of a man leaping off or on to the boat, the cable is made fast; but the man in the bows must be in readiness to haul out again on the approach of a dangerous sea, giving her cable again when the moment is favourable. By this plan, if it is properly worked, and provided the anchor holds and the cable does not part, there is no chance of the boat striking the rocks. During this operation a line should be carried from the boat's stern to the shore, so as to prevent the boat from being turned broadside on by a retiring wave. By manipulating the cable and stern line, the boat can be easily hauled backwards and forwards between her anchorage and the shore.

There are occasions when even this method puts a boat to very great risk, so that in order to communicate with the shore one has to adopt other means. Thus it happened with me when I was off the desert island of Trinidade, which is surrounded with sharp coral rocks on which breaks with fury an almost continuous surge, the rollers being sometimes of extraordinary height. On one occasion communication between the yacht and the party on shore was interrupted for several weeks by the perilous breakers. It was rare, indeed, that we ventured to beach the boat; but sometimes, when the method I have above mentioned was impracticable, a landing was effected without much risk as follows: The yacht's boat was anchored outside the surf; a line was then carried by a good swimmer, or thrown on shore, and made fast to a rock. We used to jump into the water, one at a time of course, and travel backwards and forwards, hand over hand, along this line – sometimes with small bundles of baggage or stores tied on our heads; and this with comparative ease, though the strong back undertow made it dangerous and difficult even for a powerful swimmer to attain the land. If a small craft is in danger on a surf-beaten coast, this is often the only method of safely getting her crew on shore, and there is little danger for the others if one man succeeds in getting to land with the end of the stern rope. But do not overload yourself when making such an attempt. If there is serious danger, of course nothing must be carried. I had an unpleasant experience during my first visit to Trinidade, which is described in *The Cruise of the Falcon*. I must have been somewhat imprudent in those days, for though the sea was high I put off from the shore in heavy clothes and sea-boots, loaded too with rifle, hatchet, and other articles. I leapt into the sea with a retreating wave, and proceeded to haul myself out to the boat with the line. To quote from the book: 'I was out of my depth, and I found that my impedimenta were so heavy that it was quite impossible for me to keep my head above water, and the rope was so slack that my weight at once dragged it under. I shall never forget that journey, and do not wish ever to repeat it. I was travelling under water. It was a race for life. I hauled myself up along the line as fast as my hands would move, with the energy of a drowning man. I felt as if I must have gone over a mile, and yet no boat; and indeed the distance was a very long one for a journey of this description. So long was I under water that the cook, looking on from the shore, thought I had been drowned. But at last I felt the line tighten, my head rose above the water, there was the boat just in front of me, and I scrambled on board.'

The following hints apply to river-sailing in open boats. In a river the current generally runs stronger in the centre, and more slowly along the banks; but bear in mind that, if the river is winding, the strength of the current sweeps close past the point at the convex side of each bend, and then, at first preserving its old direction, crosses diagonally towards the other side before distributing itself evenly in the channel and acquiring the direction of the new reach. On the other hand, in the bay formed on the concave side of a bend, there is little or no current, and sometimes even a back eddy will be found. When racing on a river it is important to make use of this knowledge; and also, when cruising on a river like the Seine, where the tide rushes up in a steep and dangerous wave, or *bore* as it is called in England, one's safety often depends on close attention to this tendency of river currents; for at each big bend of the river the tide is deflected, and there is generally a place on one side or the other where one can anchor in smooth water, while everywhere else the bore is breaking heavily. In straight reaches the bore is most dangerous close to the banks; at Caudebec, on the Seine, it piles up along the quay-side in a roller twenty feet in height at spring tides. If overtaken by the bore when sailing – its distant roar usually gives good warning – make for the middle of the river, lower your sail and meet it head on, pulling gently up against it with your sculls.

When turning to windward on a river, the current with you, be careful, not to tack too near in to the shore, more especially if you have not got good steerage way; for if you bring your boat within a few feet of the bank before you go about, the bow will be out of the current, while the stern, still remaining in it, will be swept up-stream, and so cause you to miss stays and probably to run on shore.

When lowering sail and taking to your oars on a river, follow the usual rule for rowing boats – that is, keep along the bank when pulling against the current; stay in mid-stream when going with it.

Beware of bridges. Do not attempt to tack through the arch of a bridge if it is a narrow one, unless you are very familiar with the conditions; it is better to lower your sail and row the boat through. Wind concentrates in an arch as in a funnel; so that supposing you approach with the wind almost abeam, you will find it suddenly head you and blow with a violent gust right in your teeth as you enter the arch. Even when running, you must be on your guard on account of this sudden great increase of the wind's strength, which is almost certain to occur; for if your mast and sail, as is often the case, will only pass narrowly under the centre of the arch, a very slight deviation from your course (almost unavoidable when a squall suddenly strikes you in the face) may cause your peak to get foul of the bridge above, when a capsize of a particularly dangerous nature is likely to ensue. Several lives of men who were good swimmers and knew their work in a boat have been lost in this way. Kew Bridge, removed last year, was not only one of the most picturesque, but was also one of the most dangerous bridges on the Thames for the boat-sailor. It crossed the river diagonally at a bend where the wind is generally shifting and squally, and where the currents form perplexing eddies.

When sailing under a bridge with a balance-lug let go the tack if there is a chance of the peak striking the bridge. This as a rule allows the yard to dip several feet, and you can quickly sweat down your tack again as soon as you have got through.

If your mast is too high to pass under a bridge, take care to lower it in good time if the current is with you. It is exceedingly awkward to find your mast jammed at the step or tabernacle, just as the stream is sweeping you on to the arch.

On several rivers special local rules are in force which, in some cases, reverse the ordinary rules of the road at sea. For example, it is the custom on many narrow rivers for a vessel tacking up against the stream to give way to a vessel running before the wind down-stream, when the two meet at a bridge which will only admit of one sailing craft at a time passing through. It is obvious that a vessel carried down by fair wind and current cannot be brought up suddenly, and would probably collide with the sides of the bridge had she to get out of the way of the vessel beating up; whereas the latter is completely under control, and can easily luff up along the bank below the bridge and wait till the other has sailed through.

It may be an unnecessary warning to give, but do not sail on the upper Thames near London, or on any other narrow crowded river, on a Bank Holiday, with a strong breeze blowing, unless you are very experienced. For an inexperienced coachman to attempt to drive a hansom through the city in the crowded hours would be rash enough, but there at any rate he would be encountering none but skilled drivers who would observe the rule of the road; whereas he who sails on the Thames through the crowd of boats collected on a public holiday must bear in mind that numbers of those who are in charge of these craft have no experience whatever of watermanship, and are wholly

ignorant of the rules of the road. Erratic often is the course
of one of these skiffs; and he or she who holds the yoke-lines,
seeing your boat rushing through the water in his direction
under a great sail, gets flurried, puts his rudder over first to
one side then to the other, gives contradictory orders to his
unmanageable crew: first they pull ahead in panic; then, just
as you prepare to pass under her stern, they of a sudden cease
rowing or back-water. You have to use all your skill and
judgment to avoid collision, and must ever be ready for any
unexpected or irrational manoeuvre on their part. I remember
once turning to windward up the river at about the same rate
that a rowing-boat was progressing in the same direction, so
that at each tack I crossed her bow or stern; her boisterous
crew of lads and damsels, to whom tacking was a mystery, took
it into their heads that I did this purposely to alarm or annoy
them, and objurgated me in emphatic terms because I did not
'sail straight, instead of zigzagging in that silly drunken fashion
from one side of the river to the other? After all, it is the holiday
of those who can go but seldom on the river, and you should
leave it to them if you can sail on other days. If you study the
happiness of the greatest number, remember that the sailing-
boat is a decided nuisance to the majority of pleasure-seekers
on the river on such an occasion.

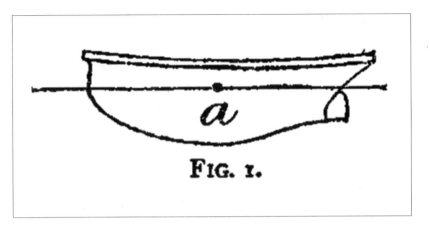

FIG. 1.

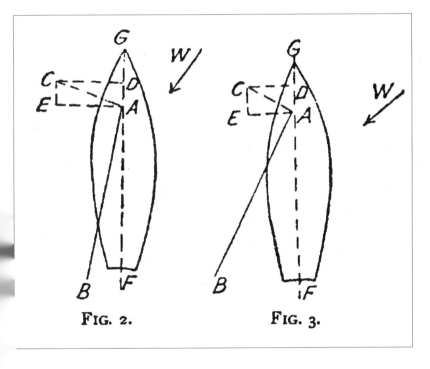

FIG. 2.   FIG. 3.

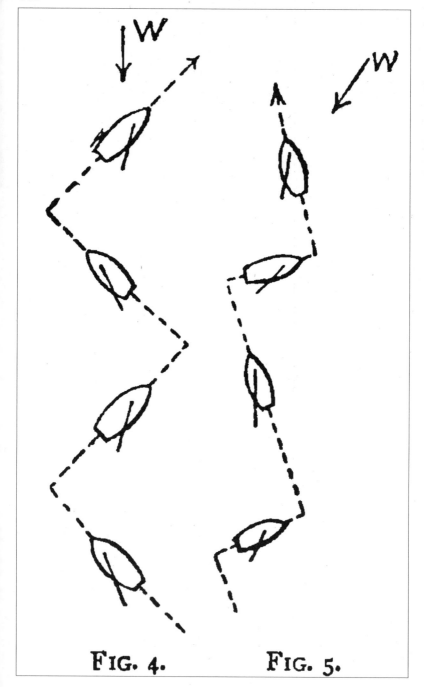

FIG. 4.   FIG. 5.

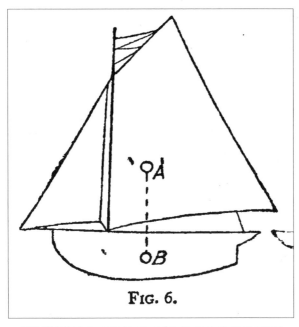

FIG. 6.

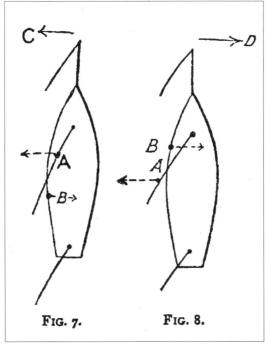

FIG. 7.

FIG. 8.

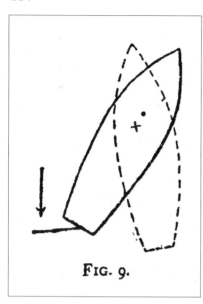

FIG. 9.

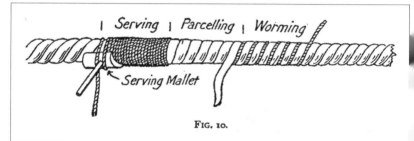

| Serving | Parcelling | Worming

Serving Mallet

FIG. 10.

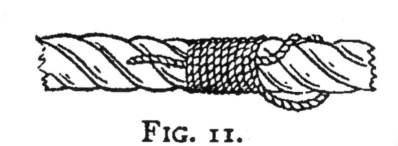

FIG. 11.

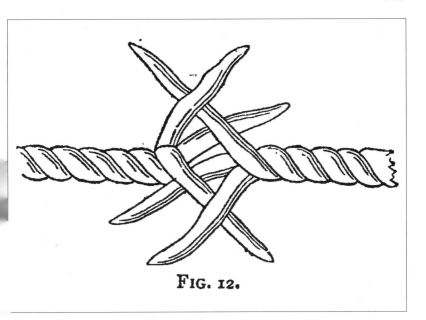

FIG. 12.

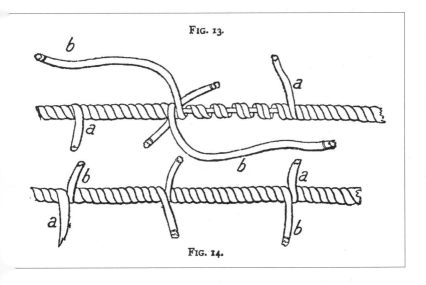

FIG. 13.

FIG. 14.

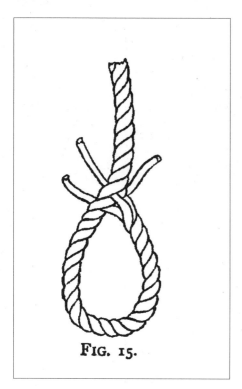

FIG. 15.

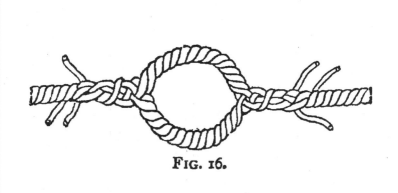

FIG. 16.

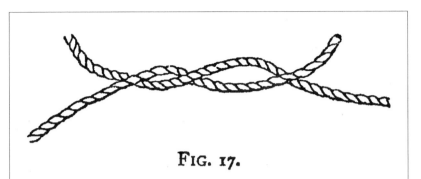

FIG. 17.

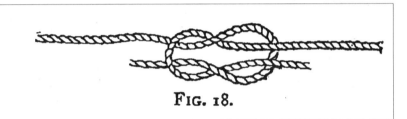

FIG. 18.

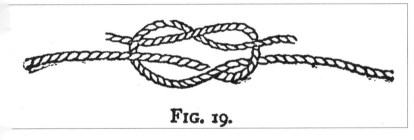

FIG. 19.

FIG. 20.

FIG. 21.

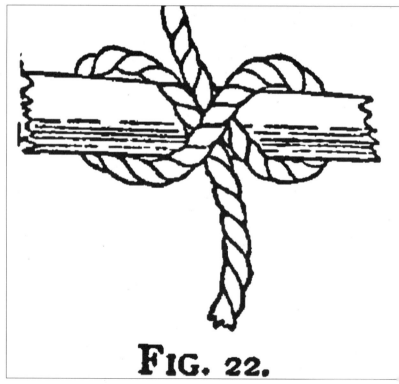

FIG. 22.

FIG. 23.

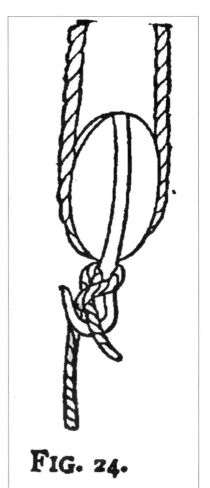

FIG. 24.

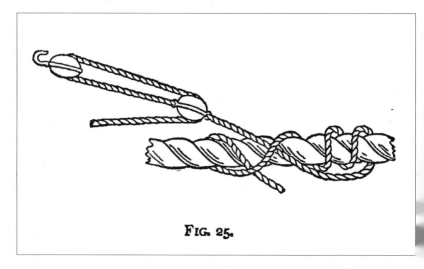

FIG. 25.

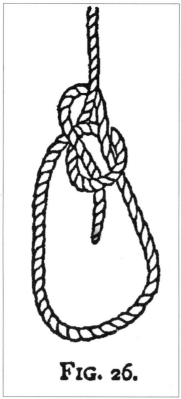

FIG. 26.

FIG. 27.

121

FIG. 28.

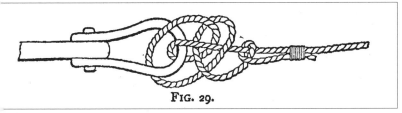

FIG. 29.

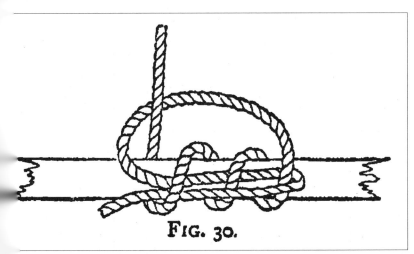

FIG. 30.

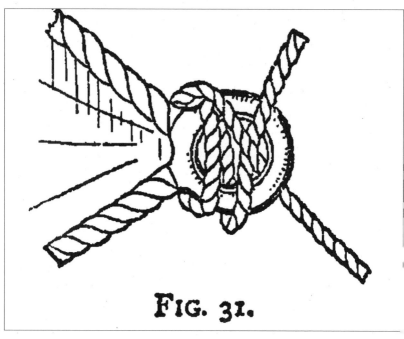

FIG. 31.

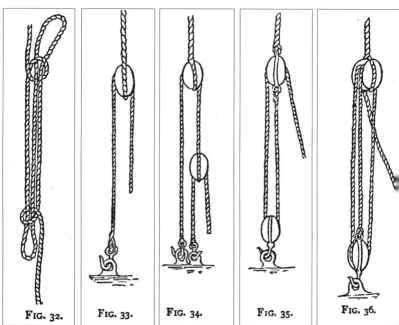

FIG. 32.   FIG. 33.   FIG. 34.   FIG. 35.   FIG. 36.

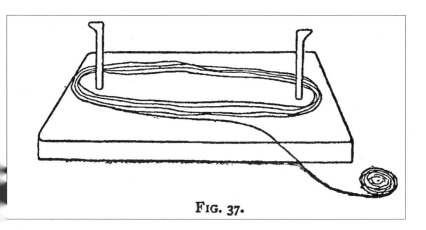

FIG. 37.

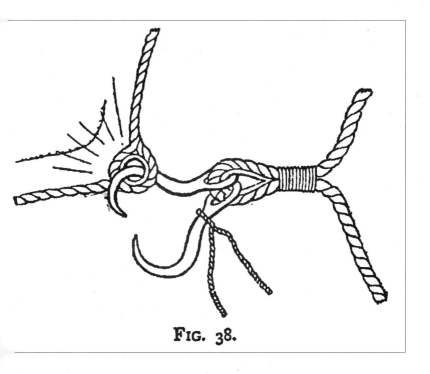

FIG. 38.

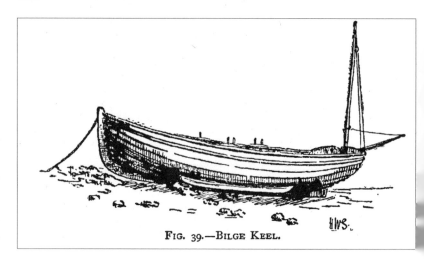

FIG. 39.—BILGE KEEL.

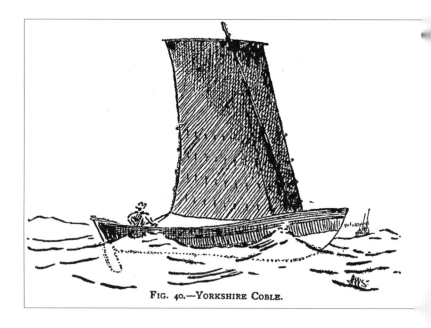

FIG. 40.—YORKSHIRE COBLE.

FIG. 41.—KETCH RIG WITH LEE-BOARDS.

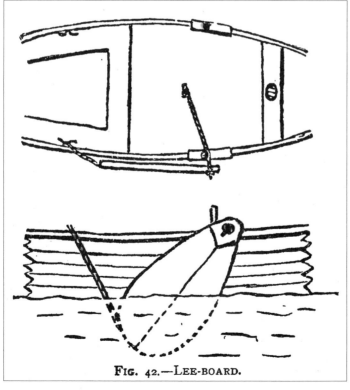

FIG. 42.—LEE-BOARD.

FIG. 43.—MOUNT'S BAY BOAT.
(DIPPING LUG MAINSAIL—STANDING LUG MIZZEN.)

FIG. 44.—STANDING LUG.

FIG. 45.—SPRITSAIL.

FIG. 46.—LEG-O'-MUTTON SAIL.

FIG. 47.—UNA BOAT.

FIG. 48.—SLIDING GUNTER.

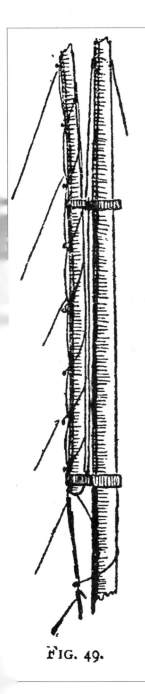

FIG. 49.

FIG. 50.

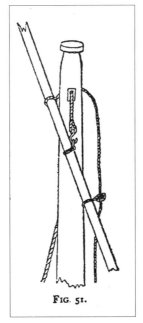

FIG. 51.

FIG. 52.—MAIN AND MIZZEN.

FIG. 53.—SLOOP.

Fig. 54.—Half-decked Boat.

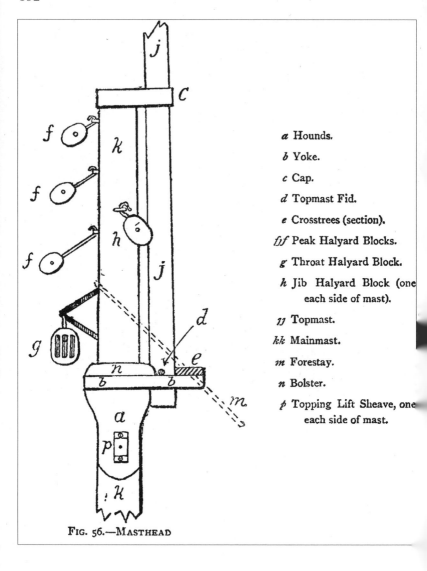

a Hounds.

b Yoke.

c Cap.

d Topmast Fid.

e Crosstrees (section).

ff Peak Halyard Blocks.

g Throat Halyard Block.

h Jib Halyard Block (one each side of mast).

jj Topmast.

kk Mainmast.

m Forestay.

n Bolster.

p Topping Lift Sheave, one each side of mast.

FIG. 56.—MASTHEAD

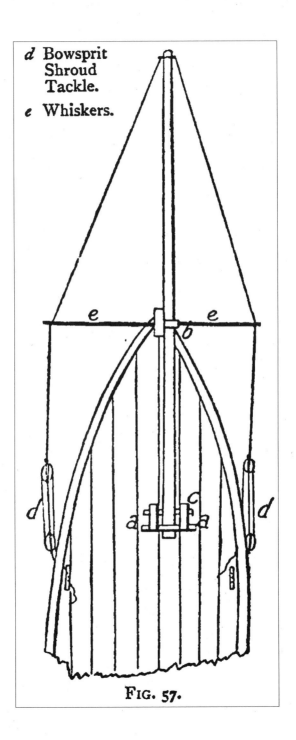

FIG. 57.

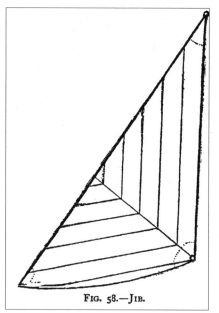

FIG. 58.—JIB.

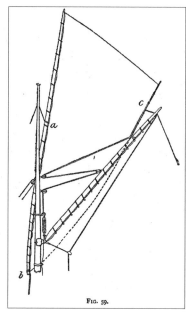

FIG. 59.

FIG. 60.—SPINNAKER TO PORT.

135

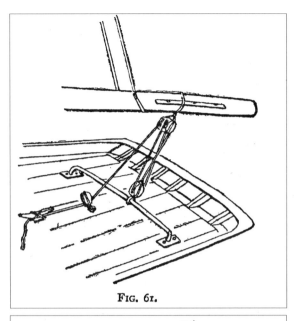

FIG. 61.

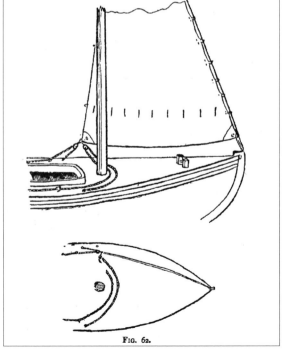

FIG. 62.

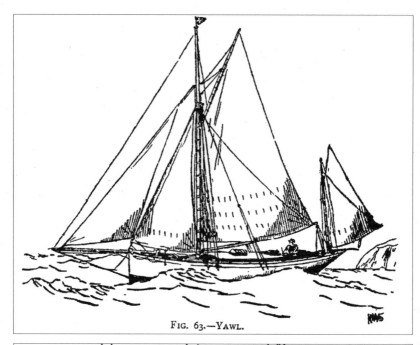

Fig. 63.—Yawl.

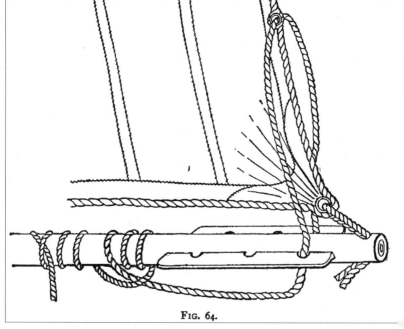

Fig. 64.

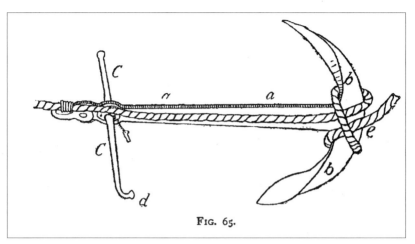

FIG. 65.

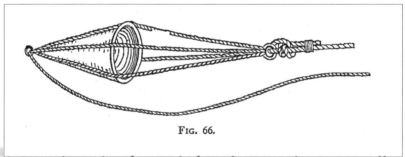

FIG. 66.

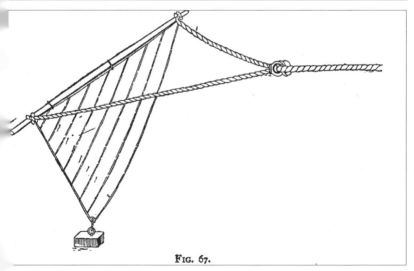

FIG. 67.

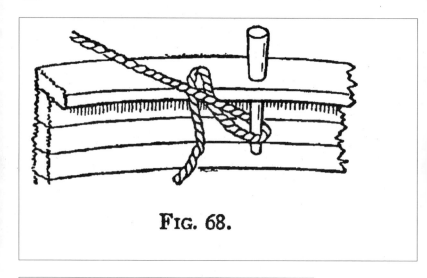

FIG. 68.

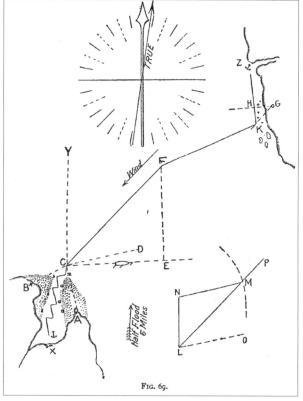

FIG. 69.

Courtesy of LoC

"BOUNCER".

"SPUNK." "LOBSTER." "KAZAZA".

The Cruising Yacht

To master the art of sailing a fore-and-after is to gain a source of much wholesome pleasure; but the pleasure is greatly enhanced when the amateur sailor has acquired sufficient knowledge to enable him to extend his sailing beyond his home waters, to cruise along shores new to him, finding his way by chart and compass, lead and log, shaping his course across broad seas with no land in sight, employing all the methods of the professional sailor. I know nothing more delightful than a summer cruise on a seaworthy little craft of the right description, oneself as skipper and a friend as crew, along the British coast with its many pleasant havens, or across the Channel to the Norman ports and up the broad Seine; or further still, beyond the North Sea, on Dutch canals and meres, through the forest-bordered sounds and up the winding fjords of Schleswig, Holstein, and Denmark; and from island to island of the clear blue Baltic Sea. One can do these things, and visit even more distant shores, with a craft of very small tonnage if she be a good sea boat and provided one does not neglect the proper precautions; it was with a three-tonner, for example, that I cruised for three summers on the rough waters of the Baltic and the North Sea without meeting with an accident of any description, though I encountered plenty of heavy weather.

The reader will have gathered from preceding chapters that the style of craft best adapted for such voyages is the beamy boat with plenty of sheer, and not carrying too much ballast – for she must be buoyant, riding comfortably and easily like a sea-bird on the tossing water, and not plunging into the crest of every wave, thereby deluging herself with water and straining every timber and spar. She should be of light draught (having a centreboard or leeboards if necessary) so that she can safely enter pleasant little shallow havens and ascend creeks and rivers closed to the deeper boat; and lastly, she should be lightly sparred and snugly canvassed, yawl or ketch rigged for choice, so that she can be easily handled. A deep-keel, narrow boat is unfitted for cruising of this sort. She is likely to be wet in a sea-way; unless provided with legs to prop her up she will heel over at a most uncomfortable angle whenever left high and dry in a tidal harbour; and – gravest objection of all – it will sometimes happen that, though bad weather is coming on, one is compelled to keep to the open sea with her and fight it out with the elements, with, nevertheless, a sheltered little harbour hard by yet inaccessible to her, into which a boat of lighter draught could have crept with ease.

The new yacht measurement rules have happily brought us back to wholesome beam. Some years ago even yachts not intended for racing were of the deep-draught, narrow-gutted description. Beam was supposed to be incompatible with speed; and yet my *Falcon* yawl, which, though only forty-two feet in length, had a beam of thirteen feet, frequently made her nine knots an hour, and on one occasion beat, I imagine, the record for vessels of her size on an ocean voyage, having sailed two thousand sea miles (from Pernambuco to Georgetown, Demerara) in ten days, running under all plain sail and spinnaker; it must be remembered, too, that she was practically jury-rigged, all her spars and sails having been cut down before I left England.

I have already said that the cruising vessel must be more lightly ballasted than the racer or the craft that is intended for sailing in some sheltered bay or river. She must not, of course, be lightened until she becomes cranky, but she should have as little ballast as possible. When fitting out my three-tonner for her Baltic cruise I took half her ballast out of her; and so, too, before sailing to the South Atlantic with the Alerte, I took out several tons of her lead ballast and substituted the same bulk of iron, the specific gravity of which is to that of lead as seven to eleven. On both these occasions my action was severely criticised by the wiseacres who hang about the shipbuilding yards; but after we had been at sea for some weeks my companions had all come round to my way of thinking.

While on the subject of ballast I may point out here that it should be stowed as snugly as possible; it should not be placed in the ends of a boat, but should be concentrated amidships, so that the vessel's bow and stern are kept buoyant, and rise readily to the seas. If the ballast is not moulded to fit to the vessel's framework, care must be taken that the pigs of iron or lead rest on the ship's timbers and not on her planking, otherwise the pressure from within will loosen the vessel's skin and render her leaky. Stow the ballast so that an open passage is left along either side of the keelson through which the bilge-water may run freely. For the same reason the limber-holes in the ship's floor timbers must be always kept clear. It is well to have a small chain rove through the limber-holes, and by occasionally drawing this backwards and forwards obstructions are removed and the water flows readily to the pump-well. The pump should be of simple construction, so that it can easily be repaired with the appliances on board. The pump-well should have a little hatch over it, so that one can quickly get access to the pump and clear it if it is choked. The above precaution is very necessary, for pumps often get out of order, especially when they are most needed. I remember well how, when my three-tonner on her way across the North Sea developed a serious leak, the pump choked after the first half-dozen strokes. On raising the pump-well hatch in the cabin floor I made a curious discovery. It would have been strange had the pump worked properly, for the well was full of wood shavings. The lazy carpenter I had employed at Hammersmith had evidently, after completing some work in the cabin, stowed the shavings in this well to save himself the trouble of throwing them overboard.

FITTING OUT FOR A CRUISE

To fit out even a small yacht for a lengthy cruise demands a good deal of consideration. In the first place, all her gear should be carefully overhauled and be replaced wherever found faulty. Two anchord should always be carried, so that the vessel can be moored with them when riding out a gale, or when the holding-ground is bad; moreover, the loss of an anchor is a contingency for which one must be prepared, and without another one to let go one may find oneself in a very awkward predicament. The first anchor, for a boat of between five and ten tons, yacht measurement, should weigh about a hundredweight.

Fifty fathoms of chain cable will suffice for it. The Trotman patent anchor is the one, in my opinion, to be preferred for a small yacht; it stows easily on deck; the arms work on a pivot in the shank; thus the arm that catches the ground is opened out and obtains a very powerful hold, while the other arm is brought close to the side of the shank, so that the chain cannot take a turn round it and foul the anchor.

The second anchor should be lighter, and for its cable a coir, or cocoanut fibre, rope can be employed with advantage. Coir rope is very light, and floats on the water; it has a great deal of spring in it, so that a vessel rides easily to it in heavy weather; for the same reason it serves well as a warp if the yacht is taken in tow by a steamer. It is often necessary to take out an anchor in the dinghy, so as to let it go at a distance from the yacht (for example, when the yacht has got aground and has to be hauled off). This can be more easily done if a coir and not a hemp rope is employed. It is also convenient to carry a small kedge anchor for anchoring temporarily, or for warping the vessel.

So as to be able to observe the Board of Trade regulations (see chapter 12), which are set out in another chapter, one must carry with one, while cruising, the red and green side-lights as prescribed in Article 2, or the combined lantern (see Article 7), and a white anchor light (see Article 11); also a bull's-eye lantern to show a light over the stern to an overtaking vessel, and so comply with Article 10. The bull's-eye should be hung up within easy reach of the helmsman; thus it can be hooked into a socket just inside the cabin door, if the boat has a well. Paraffin should be burned in these lamps, but colza is to be preferred for the binnacle lamp. It is advisable to procure lights somewhat larger than those generally supplied to small yachts, for diminutive lamps rarely burn well. A fog-horn – one of the ordinary horns sounded with the mouth satisfies the new Board of Trade rules for yachts under twenty tons – and a bell must be carried, with which to signal in thick weather. The rules for employing them will be set forth in another, chapter.

A good compass is of course indispensable. On a small cruising yacht it should be secured on the fore-side of the well on a level with the deck, or in some other position where it can be plainly seen by the helmsman, and it should be as far removed as possible from the local attraction of ballast, large bolts, or other iron. The Mariner's Compass is too well known to need minute description here. The compass-card, divided into the thirty-two points of the compass, turns freely on a pivot fixed in the centre of the compass-bowl, the bowl being hung on double gimbals in the binnacle, so that it remains horizontal though the vessel rolls and pitches. On the side of the binnacle is a small oil lamp which lights the compass-card by night. When the steering compass is in position, the Lubber's Line (a vertical mark on the compass-bowl) must be pointing directly towards the ship's head. Consequently, the point on the compass-card which is in line with the lubber's line shows the direction by compass of the ship's head. What is known as the liquid compass is the best for a small yacht – that is, one in which the bowl is filled with spirit or glycerine, so as to retard the motion of the compass-card; for the violent jumping of a little boat in a sea-way is apt to make the ordinary compass-card swing and spin round so that it becomes impossible to steer by it. Even when a liquid compass is used the card is often very unsteady; in that case watch the points on the card as they swing past the lubber's line. The mean between the extreme points reached will be the direction of the vessel's head.

Before one sets out on a cruise the vessel should be 'swung' to ascertain if there be any deviation of the compass – that is, error due to the local attraction of the ballast or other iron on board. The yacht should be swung when she is at her moorings. In the first place, the correct compass-bearings of some distant object should be ascertained. This can be done by means of a compass raised to such a height above the deck as to be beyond all local attraction; or, if the exact position of the vessel is known, the bearings of some known object (a lighthouse, for example) can be found by reference to a chart. The object must be sufficiently far off – say, at three miles – so that the bearing will not appreciably · alter as the vessel swings. Then by slowly carrying the cable or mooring-rope down one side of the vessel to her stern and back to the bow along the other side, the tide can be made to swing her right round; or if there is no tide her head can be gently pulled round with the dinghy; or again, if one is not pressed for time, one can make one's observations for deviation as the vessel swings naturally to ebb and flow. As her head is brought in succession on to each of the thirty-two points of the compass, careful bearings of the object must be taken – the compass, of course, being stationed in the exact position in which it will be used at sea. If all the bearings agree with each other and with the correct bearings, there is no deviation; but if they differ, a table must be drawn up showing the exact deviation for each point of the compass towards which the vessel's bow was directed; and when shaping one's course at sea this table must be referred to, and proper allowance must be made for the error. The rule is – with westerly deviation allow to the left, and with easterly deviation to the right. For example, if one desires to sail N.E., and the table shows that with the vessel's head pointing N.E. her compass has an easterly deviation of one point, one will have to steer one point to the left of N.E. – that is, N.E. by N.

The following example will show how a Deviation Table is drawn up. The deviation for the first four points only out of the thirty-two is given:

The table is thus employed. Look to column 3 for the direction in which you wish to sail; the corresponding course in Table 1 is the course which you must steer by your compass. For example, by the table above, if your destination bears N.E. you will have to steer N. by your compass. The points of the compass are generally expressed in degrees on a Deviation Table. (As there are thirty-two points in the circle of 360 degrees, a point measures 11¼ degrees.) Thus N.E. would be N. 45 degrees E. But when navigating a small yacht it is unnecessary to employ these numerical subdivisions of the points of the compass; the quarter-point is a sufficiently minute division for all practical purposes. On small wooden yachts, if the compass is in the right place and proper precautions are taken, there is rarely any serious deviation.

Among the many articles that one must not forget to have on board when fitting out for a foreign cruise are marline-spikes; carpenter's tools; spare blocks, thimbles, and shackles; buckets, brooms, and mops; spare crutches for the dinghy; needles and palm for repairing sails; tarred twine; spare ropes; paint-brushes; tins of paint and varnish. One should carry strong fenders with which to protect the vessel's side when she is lying alongside a quay. The fenders sold by the yachting fitters look very smart in their white coats, but they will not stand much rough work. It is better to make one's own fenders; a few lengths of coir rope neatly seized together form a very efficient fender. See that you supply yourself with the above and other requirements before you sail from England; for you will have to pay much more for them if you do your purchasing at a ship-chandler's in a foreign port. The same rule applies to tinned meats and other non-perishable provisions.

The cooking-stove is not the least important item on the yacht's inventory. A charcoal stove is the best if one is cruising in chilly autumn or winter weather, as it will keep the cabin warm. But a spirit or paraffin stove is much the more convenient for summer work, as it can be lighted in a moment when required, and extinguished as quickly when it has done its work. The spirit stove, on account of its superior cleanliness, is, in my opinion, far to be preferred to that which burns paraffin. The latter, unless very carefully tended, produces lamp-black, than which no form of dirt is more difficult to deal with on board a boat. Throughout my South American and West Indian cruises on the *Falcon*, and my voyages on smaller craft on the Baltic and nearer waters, I employed nothing but a spirit stove. The expense is moderate. There is never any difficulty in renewing one's supply of spirit. At every little home port one can procure methylated spirits; and in every foreign port I have visited spirits of wine, or some other form of alcohol, are to be purchased at small cost. On referring to my log, I find that on my Baltic cruise, though we did a good deal of cooking, we consumed only a shilling's worth of spirit a week.

The internal or domestic arrangements of the cruising yacht will depend much upon the individual tastes of the owner. The cabin of the little five-tonner can be made very comfortable, and it is well to have it so if it is to be one's home for several weeks or months. It should be provided with cupboards in which to keep such articles as would be spoiled by damp, and with lockers along the sides under the bunks, where bottles of beer and other stores that will not be affected by water can be stowed. On the walls there should be racks for glasses, shelves for books, and nettings for charts, etc. Everything must have its right place on a boat, not only on deck, but below as well; for not to be able to put one's hand in a moment on the dividers and parallel rules, or even, say, the corkscrew, is almost as bad as to have to fumble about in search of a halyard which has been belayed to a wrong cleat. When upholstering the cabin, bear in mind that sea-water is likely to get into it now and again, so do not cover your bunks with materials whose colour is likely to wash out; dark flannel makes the best colour for the bunks, and is not cold to sleep on like American cloth. The floor carpeting should be capable of being easily washed and rapidly dried; for a small yacht nothing is so good as cocoanut matting.

In the forecastle of the small cruiser are kept the stove and cooking-pots, the lamps, mops, brooms, and so forth. On some boats the spare sails are kept here, and one's oilskins can hang on the walls. The chain-locker is also in the forecastle. If the chain is a long one it should be divided into two or more lengths, which can be connected when necessary by shackles. In the chain-locker should be stowed a length of chain sufficient for ordinary working purposes. The rest of the chain can be stowed under the cabin flooring on the top of the ballast, to be brought out and shackled on to the working chain when heavy weather or bad holding-ground necessitate riding to a long scope of cable. To have all one's chain in the locker is to carry superfluous weight in the very place where it should not be, in the bows of the vessel, where it tends to drag her nose down, prevents her rising to the waves, and makes her a wet and uncomfortable boat in a sea-way. It is not often that one has to employ more than twenty-five fathoms of chain when anchoring a five-tonner, as one can generally creep into shallow water for a berth; therefore it is not necessary to carry a greater length than this in the sail-locker.

On a boat of under five tons measurement the anchor can be got up by hand; so it is well to dispense with a windlass, and thus avoid an extra weight in the bows. If the anchor ever gets such firm hold of the ground that it will not come up, a watch tackle clapped on to the chain will generally dislodge it. If no windlass is carried, it is essential that the chain end should be made fast to a bolt in one of the forecastle timbers, or other secure place, else some careless person may, when anchoring, let the whole chain run overboard. Indeed, this precaution should be taken even if a windlass is employed.

Capacious lockers generally surround the small yacht's well. In one of these the spare sails can be kept, in another the warps, spare blocks, etc., while another will serve as larder. A completely watertight well adds greatly to the cruiser's safety. It should be provided with a powerful well-pump so that it can be quickly emptied if a sea be shipped.

THE YACHT'S DINGHY

Every cruising yacht must have with her a dinghy of some description. It is almost im-possible to carry a wooden dinghy on the deck of a small yacht; as a rule, therefore, the boat has to be towed astern, retarding the vessel's speed considerably, and becoming a source of danger in rough water. If too long a tow-line is given to a dinghy when running before a heavy sea she will steer wildly, alternately leaping her whole painter's length down upon the vessel, and drifting astern again till the tautening line brings her up with another jerk. She is very likely in these circumstances either to stave herself in or to drive a hole in the vessel's stern, and she is all the more likely to come to grief if the yacht has a long counter. The best plan in heavy weather is to tow the dinghy with two very short tow-lines, one fastened to each of the vessel's quarters; this will prevent her from sheering about, and, even if she does strike the vessel occasionally, she will do so with no great force. If a weight is put in her stern, she will steer better still. I towed a wooden dinghy from the Thames to Sweden and back again behind my three-ton ketch (which I have described in a former chapter), frequently encountering bad weather on both the North Sea and the Baltic, without the boat's suffering any injury. But the ketch, it must be remembered, was an old P. and O. lifeboat and had a pointed stern, so that if the dinghy's bow struck her it glided off instead of delivering a heavy blow, as would have been the case had the vessel had a square stern or a counter. Moreover, the dinghy had a small false keel, and with this a boat always steers much more steadily.

A collapsible dinghy is undoubtedly the best for a small yacht, as it can be folded up and laid on deck, or can even be stowed away in the cabin. The Berthon collapsible boat, of which I have had considerable experience, is a very good sea-boat. Though made of canvas, one can take a Berthon through a surf and beach her on a rocky shore without tearing her frail sides if proper precautions are taken; indeed a light Berthon, with a couple of active men in charge, runs less risk of having a hole knocked into her bottom than does a heavy wooden boat. I had a ten-foot Berthon with me on the Falcon during my cruise in South American waters, and I have often landed her safely on a shore bristling with sharp coral rocks. The procedure was as follows: on getting into the breakers my companion and myself would jump overboard – possibly to find ourselves out of our depth – and holding on to her, one on each side, we would take her on with us, wading or swimming, lift her up bodily when in shallow water, carry her above the reach of the breakers, and then lay her gently down. We used to put off from the shore in the same fashion; that is, we would wade in quickly after a retiring wave, carrying the Berthon with us, swim out with her till we were outside the breakers, and then in turn clamber on board over the stern. The James collapsible boat is also highly spoken of by those who have used it, and it certainly looks like a very serviceable yacht's dinghy.

It is always well to have a mast and sail for one's dinghy. The pleasures of yachting are much enhanced if one carries a boat with which one can sail while the vessel lies at anchor, for one can then make many interesting little voyages on waters inaccessible to the yacht. If one decides to tow a wooden dinghy astern she can be fitted with a wooden centreboard or with a false keel, to enable her to turn to windward, for this does not materially increase her weight. The dinghy I had with me while cruising on the Baltic was eleven feet long; she had a false keel nearly six inches deep, and a large balance-lug under which she sailed very well. I have many pleasant memories of my wanderings with her up sheltered inland waters – streams, creeks, and meres – while the wind and sea were roaring outside the harbour where the yacht lay weather-bound. The dinghy would be brought alongside; the mast, the sail, and a few pigs of ballast would be lowered into her; a provision of bread and cheese and beer would be placed in the stern-sheets, pipe and tobacco would not be forgotten; and then, with sketch-book and fishing-rod as my companions, away I would sail for the whole long summer day. One day, for example, starting from the entrance of the Slei Fjord, where the yacht lay at anchor, I sailed up that winding water to Schleswig and back, a cruise of sixty miles of the yacht by the action of the current, and at the next is blown towards her by a stronger puff than usual. When a dinghy behaves in this fashion fasten a bucket to her stern by a line about six feet long, and let the bucket sink in the water; the pressure exerted on the bucket by the tide will drag the dinghy astern and keep her away from the yacht.

10

The Art of Coasting

A yacht of small tonnage, such as I have described in this book, is unfit for an ocean voyage; but, as I have already said, she can be safely navigated from one end of Europe to the other, provided she be a boat of the right sort, and the skipper knows his business and is not foolhardy. 'Coasting' is a wide term, and to cross the North Sea where it is four hundred miles in breadth would still be reckoned as coasting work. On a coasting voyage to the Baltic, for example, one would often be out of sight of land for many hours at a time. A knowledge of navigation in the strict sense of the term – that is, the determination of a vessel's position at sea by observation of the sun, moon, and stars, and her guidance from land to land by dead reckoning, as carried out in the orthodox fashion by working traverses, and so forth – is not needed by the coasting seaman. A rough-and-ready system suffices for the little cruiser; but as her owner has to pick his way along, to him, unfamiliar coasts, identifying new landmarks, avoiding shoals and rocks and other dangers, shaping his course across broad waters, he must carry with him certain instruments and other articles connected with navigation, and make himself thoroughly conversant with their use. Thus he must provide himself with a hand-lead and line for sounding; a log-ship and line with which to gauge the speed his vessel is making; the charts of the coasts he proposes to visit, and the pilot-books and sailing directions to accompany them; dividers and parallel rules; and one of the almanacs published for the use of the coasting sailor (Pearson's is the one which I have always used, and it is to be highly recommended) which contain the tide-tables for British and other European ports, and a good deal of other useful information.

THE CHART

As the world is spherical, no portion of it can be correctly represented on a flat surface such as a chart. All maps and charts necessarily distort the relative sizes of different regions and the distances between various points. Several methods of dealing with this difficulty have been devised. Formerly mariners employed the Plane Chart, on which the parallels of latitude and the meridians of longitude were drawn as equidistant straight lines. This was correct so far as the parallels of latitude are concerned; but whereas the meridians of longitude are in fact furthest apart at the Equator and meet at the Poles, great error was produced by this projection. At last Kauffman, known as Mercator, introduced the chart called after him Mercator's Chart, which was at once recognised as being admirably adapted for the purposes of navigation. In the Mercator's chart, as in the Plane chart, the meridians of longitude are drawn as parallel equidistant straight lines; they are thus greatly distorted, and the Polar regions are magnified to an enormous extent; but the parallels of latitude are not drawn as equidistant, as in the Plane Chart, but are distorted in proportion to the distortion of the meridians – that is, they are drawn further apart as the Poles are approached. For example, a degree of longitude on the latitude of Edinburgh, though appearing on Mercator's Chart of the same length as a degree of longitude at the Equator, is in reality nearly double the length of the latter: a degree of latitude on the parallel of Edinburgh – as will be seen on inspecting a chart – is therefore magnified in like proportion, being drawn nearly twice as long as a degree of latitude on the Equator. By this projection, consequently, the relative shape of different regions of the Earth is approximately preserved.

The great advantage of Mercator's Chart lies in the fact that, though upon it there is a distortion of relative magnitudes and distances, the direction from one point to another is correctly represented; that is, if a place is N.N.E. of another place it appears so on the chart, and a straight line drawn on a chart between the two places would correctly represent the track of a vessel steering on a N.N.E. course. The mariner can therefore find his course from one place to another without any difficulty on this chart. The parallel rules are laid so that one edge touches both places on the chart; the rules are then slid over the surface of the chart (one of the rules only being moved at a time, so that the direction is preserved) until one edge is exactly over the centre of one of the compasses which are designed on the chart. The edge will then indicate on the compass the course to be steered.

Except in certain special plans, which, for convenience, are drawn on a diagonal scale, the top of a chart is the true North, the bottom is the true South, and the right and left sides are true East and West respectively; straight parallel lines drawn across the chart from right to left and from top to bottom representing the parallels of latitude and the meridians of longitude. I need scarcely explain that the magnetic needle, in most parts of the world, does not point due North, but to the West or East of it at an angle which varies with the locality. The difference between the true and magnetic North is called the Variation of the Compass, and is expressed in its angular value; thus, outside the mouth of the English Channel, the variation is 25 degrees W. The compasses designed on general charts, such as the chart of the North Atlantic, show the true points of the compass, but on the coasting charts employed by the owner of the small cruiser the compass designs are more generally magnetic. When laying down one's course on a chart of the latter description, one has but to use the parallel rules in the manner I have already explained, and the course to be steered will be read off on the compass design. On the other hand if one is using a chart on which the compass is true, one must correct for variation the course as shown on the chart. The variation is given in figures on most charts. When correcting a true course into a magnetic course, allowance to the right must be made if the variation is westerly, to the left if it is easterly. For example, if one's true course by the chart is S.W. and the variation is 25 degrees W., one must steer 25 degrees – that is, roughly, two points – to the right of S.W., which makes the course W.S.W.

Not only can one find one's correct course on a chart, but it is also possible, despite the distortion of magnitudes produced by Mercator's projection, to measure distances upon it. To do this with accuracy necessitates calculations beyond the scope of this book; these are explained in Norie's, Raper's, and other works on navigation. But distances can also be approximately ascertained on the chart by simple measurement, a method sufficiently accurate for all practical purposes. On looking at a chart it will be seen that the lines representing the meridians on the extreme right and left are graduated, that is, marked off in degrees and minutes of latitude. These graduated meridians can be used as a scale for the measurement of distance upon the chart. But as degrees of latitude, though everywhere of equal length, on Mercator's chart are drawn longer as the poles are approached, each particular section of the graduated meridian can only serve as a scale for the regions on that latitude.

Thus if we wish to measure the distance between two places on the chart, one of which is in 50 degrees North latitude and the other in 60 degrees North, we must use as scale of miles that part of the graduated meridian lying between those limits. The following is the quickest method of procedure. Open the dividers so that the two legs are on the two places on the chart. Then with the dividers measure off this distance on the graduated meridians, so placing the dividers that the mean latitude between the two places (which would be 55 degrees North in the above example) lies half-way between the two legs of the dividers. The distance can now be read off the graduated meridian, in degrees and minutes, a degree containing 60 minutes or nautical miles, which are to English miles roughly as seven are to six. On coasting charts, where small areas only are represented, an ordinary scale of nautical miles is sometimes drawn, which serves to measure distances with sufficient accuracy.

In addition to its accurate representation of the configuration of the coast, a chart supplies the mariner with a variety of necessary information. The signs and abbreviations employed are usually explained in the corner of the chart. The following are the most important among these:

The small numbers on a chart indicate the soundings, either in fathoms or feet, at low water ordinary spring tides. The nature of the bottom is also shown, the following being some of the abbreviations used: *cl.*, clay; *c.*, coarse; *f.*, fine; *g.*, gravel; *h.*, hard; *s.*, soft; *m.*, mud; *oz.*, ooze; *peb.*, pebbles; *sk.*, shells.

The Roman numerals on the chart give the Tidal Establishment of the place; that is, the hour of high water at the full and change of the moon. Thus H. W. F. & C. XIh. 40m., signifies high water at full and change at eleven hours forty minutes. From this one is able by the following method, without any reference to tide tables, to calculate with sufficient accuracy the hour of high water. Find in your almanac the date of the last full or new moon, and for every day that has elapsed since then add forty-eight minutes to the time of high-water at full and change, as given on the chart.

Arrows on the chart indicate the direction of tides and currents: on some charts an arrow feathered on one side shows the direction of the flood-tide, an unfeathered arrow that of the ebb.

The rate of tides and currents is given in knots and fractions of knots. The rise of the tide is given in feet.

The qualities of the lights displayed on lighthouses and light-ships are shown as follows on the chart: *Lt. F.*, light fixed; *Lt. Fl*, light flashing; *Lt. Rev.*, light revolving. The intervals between flashes; the durations of revolutions; the colour of lights; the radius at which a light is visible in ordinary weather from a ship's deck; the different bearings between which a light becomes visible, or is obscured, or shows a different colour, etc., are also indicated on the chart.

The following abbreviations, among others, are employed to show the distinguishing marks and colours of buoys and

Deacons, etc.: *B.*, black; *R.*, red; *W.*, white; *H. S.*, horizontally striped; *V. S.*, vertically striped; *Cheq.*, chequered; *B. R.*, black and red.

SOUNDING

A Lead and Line for sounding are indispensable on every yacht. For a small cruiser the deep-sea-lead, weighing 28 pounds, is of course unnecessary; the hand lead of 14 pounds, is sufficient; and even a lighter lead, say of five pounds, will as a rule be found the most convenient for coasting purposes.

The line generally used with the hand lead is twenty-five fathoms long, and is marked at intervals in the following manner:

> At 2 fathoms with leather with two ends; at 3 fathoms with leather with three ends; at 5 fathoms with white calico; at 7 fathoms with red bunting; at 10 fathoms with leather with a whole in it; at 13 fathoms with blue serge; at 15 fathoms with white calico; at 17 fathoms with red bunting; at 20 fathoms with strand with two knots in it.

These marks make it easy to distinguish the depth of water when sounding by day; and, at night, the leadsman can tell by the different feel of the materials used for the marks which one is passing through his hand. The intervening unmarked depths in fathoms are called the deeps; of these there are therefore eleven, as follows: 1, 4, 6, 8, 9, 11, 12, 14, 16, 18, and 19 fathoms.

In order to take soundings from a vessel which is under way, hold the line in the hand about six feet from the lead; swing the lead round to give it momentum, and throw it forward so that it falls in the water in front of the vessel. The advance of the vessel will bring the line almost perpendicularly over the lead; take in the slack of the line so soon as the absence of weight shows you that the lead has reached the bottom; and then the portion of the line on the surface of the water will indicate the 203 depth. In order to obtain an accurate sounding, all this must be done smartly, more especially if the vessel has much speed on her. It is often advisable to heave the vessel to while sounding.

It is the custom at sea for the leadsman after taking a cast of the lead to sing out the depth in marks and deeps. Thus if the first piece of red bunting is on the surface of the water, indicating a depth of seven fathoms, he calls out 'By the mark seven!' If the five-fathom mark is submerged and the seven-fathom mark is six feet out of the water, he calls out 'By the deep six!' The depths are calculated to quarter fathoms; thus if the depth be a quarter of a fathom more than six fathoms, this would be announced by the leadsman as 'By the deep six, and a quarter six!'

Always take soundings on the windward side of a vessel: if you throw the lead over on the lee side, the leeway of the vessel will cause her to drift across your line, which may consequently get foul of keel or rudder.

There is a hollow at the heel of a lead, and if this be filled with tallow (the process is called 'arming the lead') a cast of the lead brings up a specimen of the bottom, mud, gravel, shells, as the case may be. This is often of great service – in foggy weather, for example, when landmarks are not distinguishable – for if one compares the depth of water and nature of the bottom as given by the lead with the similar indications on the chart, the position of the vessel may be ascertained. Allowance must of course be made for the state of the tide; the soundings on the charts, as I have already explained, being calculated for low water, ordinary spring tides.

The log-ship, log-line, and log-glass enable one to calculate a vessel's speed through the water. The log-ship is a triangular piece of wood, about five inches broad, weighted with lead on one side so as to sink it and keep it perpendicular. The end of the log-line is attached to the corners of the log-ship by three small lines, forming a bridle. One of these lines terminates in a peg which fits into a hole in the log-ship, in such a way that it is released when a strain is put on the log-ship; the log-ship then being turned on edge, offers small resistance to the water, and can be more easily hauled on board.

The Log-Glass is a common sand-glass constructed so as to run out in a certain number of seconds – generally fifteen or thirty seconds.

The Log-line, which is 120 fathoms long, is knotted at regular intervals, the distances between knot and knot bearing the same proportion to a nautical mile as the number of seconds in which the glass runs out bears to one hour. The last few fathoms of line next to the log-ship are not knotted, and this portion, known as the stray-line, is marked by a bit of bunting. The log-line is wound round a reel.

The log is hove in the following way: One man takes the reel in his hand while another holds the log-glass upright, with all the sand lying in the lower cup. When the word is given the log-ship is thrown overboard and drops astern. The moment that the bunting, marking the end of the stray-line, is seen to go over the quarter, the order turn is given and the man holding the glass reverses it so that the sand begins to run. The log-ship, owing to the resistance of the water, drags the line out from the reel. As the last sand runs out of the upper cup of the glass, the man holding it calls stop. The line is immediately checked, and the number of knots that have gone overboard show the number of nautical miles or knots per hour that the vessel is making through the water. The check on the line at the end of the operation releases the bridle-peg of which I have spoken, so that the log-ship is now easily hauled on board.

The patent self-registering logs are scarcely to be recommended for small craft. Though answering excellently on steamers, they are apt to register a less distance than has in reality been made if a vessel is sailing slowly in light winds. After some practice the yachtsman should be able, by looking at the water over the side, to gauge pretty accurately the rate at which his little craft is going; and it is rare indeed, even in the course of a long coasting voyage, that he will find it necessary to use a log of any description – at any rate that is my experience.

TIDES

I have already explained how one can calculate the hour of high water at a place for any particular day, if the chart indicates the tidal establishment of that place – that is, the hour of high water there; at the full and change of the moon. But a more acccurate method for finding the time of high water for any well-known port is to refer to a Nautical Almanac, such as Pearson's, which costs only sixpence, and is the most useful little book of its kind I know of. In this almanac are to be found tide tables for some of the principal ports in Great Britain, and also an extensive list of British and other ports and positions with their tidal constants – that is, the difference in time between the high water at these places and high water at some standard port, such as London Bridge.

Thus if you wish to ascertain the time of high water at the Nore for August 15, refer to the above-mentioned list and you will find that the tidal constant for the Nore is – 1h. 45m., which signifies that it is high water there one hour and forty-five minutes earlier than at London Bridge. Then look up the London Bridge tide tables for the hour of high water on August 15, which we will suppose to be 3h. 15m. p.m. Deduct 1h. 45m. from 3h. 15m., and the result, 1h. 30m. p.m., will be the time of high water at the Nore for that day. If the sign before the constant had been + instead of – it would have signified that it was high water at the Nore later than at London Bridge, and you would have had to add the times instead of subtracting one from the other.

When the tidal constant of a place is not given in the almanac, it can be found, provided one knows the tidal establishment of the place and also that of some standard port, e.g. London Bridge; for the difference between these two times is the tidal constant of the place, additive if the tidal establishment of the place is greater than that of London, subtractive if it be less. Thus if the chart gives the tidal establishment of the place as IVh., the difference between IVh. and Ih. 58m. (which is the tidal establishment of London Bridge) gives the tidal constant + 2h. 2m., which can be applied to the London Bridge tide tables, in the manner before explained, in order to find the hour of high water for the day.

It must be borne in mind that strong winds often accelerate or retard high water and affect the range of the tide. Thus on the Thames, with a gale from the East, high water will be earlier and the rise of the tide will be higher than would be the case if the conditions were normal.

When shaping one's course at sea and establishing one's position in the manner that will be explained in the next chapter, it is often of great importance to know at what hour the tide turns and at what speed it runs at different periods of the flood and ebb. In the first place, in the open sea, the tide rises from low to high water in about six hours and twelve minutes, and falls from high to low water in the same time. Near the land various conditions affect the tide, and on tidal rivers the further one is above the mouth the shorter is the duration of the flood. Thus on the Thames at Kew the tide flows for about three hours only, while the current is running down for about nine hours.

The tide rises fastest at half-flood and is at its slowest during the first and last hours of the flood. On the average, if x represent the rise of the tide in feet during the first hour of the flood $3x$ will be the rise in the second hour, $4x$ in the third hour, $4x$ in the fourth hour, $3x$ in the fifth hour, and x in the last hour. The rate of the ebb is in the reverse order.

THE BAROMETER

Of all the articles that are required for the equipment of the small cruising vessel none is more indispensable than the aneroid barometer. The little cutter or yawl of five tons is not intended to contend with strong gales at sea. In the course of a long coasting voyage, such as to the Baltic, one is sure to encounter rough weather occasionally; but it is almost certain to be through one's own fault if one is caught out at sea in a dangerous storm. For him who can read his barometer aright and does not neglect its warnings, there is no foolhardiness in coasting all over Europe with a small craft. A coasting voyage of this description is a succession of comparatively short runs from port to port; and it is seldom that one is compelled to be as much as twenty-four hours at a time at sea. The prudent mariner picks his weather before leaving the shelter of a port, to make a passage of any duration. He awaits a 'slant' as the sailors call it – that is, steady fine weather and a fair wind. When he is assured of these conditions by the indications of his barometer and other favourable signs, he weighs his anchor and speeds to the harbour of his destination, his object being to get there as soon as possible and before the weather can undergo a change for the worse.

Dangerous weather very rarely, if ever, comes on unheralded, and if one awaits the right moment one can practically insure for oneself fine weather for at least twenty-four hours. I have sometimes been kept in port unnecessarily by an unfavourable weather forecast, the expected gale not arriving; but I cannot call to mind any occasion on which really bad weather has come when the barometer has foretold that it would be fine. Before sailing from a British port one should read the weather observations in one of the morning papers. Each leading London paper publishes a chart representing the movement of the barometer for several days, and also the forecast for twenty-four hours, for different districts, which is issued each night by the Meteorological Office.

A friend of mine, a most skilled yachtsman in most respects, once sailed from the Isle of Wight to Havre in his five-tonner. He was caught in a gale before he made his port, lost his dinghy, and very nearly lost his vessel and his life. I heard the Cowes boatmen speaking of his foolhardiness in crossing the Channel, where it is one hundred miles broad, with so small a craft. Now they were wrong in making this criticism; for it was not in attempting the passage that his foolhardiness lay, but in his neglect to look at his barometer before he weighed his anchor. He was too impatient to await a slant. I have myself undertaken numerous long coasting voyages with five-tonners, three-tonners, and open boats, having sailed many thousands of miles on the waters that wash our own shores, on the Baltic, the Carribean and other seas, and I do not consider that I was guilty of any foolhardiness in doing so; but had it not been that I always carefully picked my weather and watched my glass, I should no doubt have come to grief time after time. It is the cautious and not the reckless sailor who takes his little vessel to distant shores; for the reckless one, if he attempts the foreign cruise, is likely to have such unpleasant experiences before he has got far from home that he will abandon his enterprise, and may consider himself lucky if he succeeds in bringing his vessel back to his starting-point. Have you not always observed that the reckless person, who undertakes some risky adventure in thoughtless ignorance, is the first to lose his head in the presence of the danger, which he was unable to realise before he blindly rushed into it?

Some people place implicit faith in the weather wisdom of old sailors. This is all very well in its way, and weather can, of course, be foretold by observing the aspect of the sky, the movements of birds, and so forth. But I have often found the old sailor altogether at fault in his prognostications: the barometer is the only reliable guide. In *The Falcon on the Baltic* I illustrated these truths by narrating my own experiences on two occasions. On the first occasion I was lying weather-bound in Harwich waiting for a slant to take me to Holland. It was wild-looking weather, the boatmen of the place shook their heads knowingly, and were confident that a storm was on its way to us, and the coxswain of the lifeboat told me that a friend of his, the skipper of a barge, had telegraphed from South Shields – 'Barge detained by heavy gales.' But I could not believe that my barometer, which had been steady for some days, was capable of deceiving me; and moreover the wind was fair, so I was inclined to be off. However, so as to satisfy my mind, I decided to obtain a later official forecast than that afforded by the morning papers. I remembered that the Meteorological Office would, if applied to, telegraph a weather-forecast for the sum of one shilling. So I availed myself of this very useful arrangement. I telegraphed in the afternoon, 'What weather Harwich to Rotterdam to-morrow?' in an hour's time I received the following reply: 'Light S.W. breezes, fine, sea nearly smooth.' I knew that the official opinion of the clerk of the weather was more to be relied on than the wisdom of all the ancient mariners put together; so despite the stormy-looking sky and the warnings of wiseacres on shore, I weighed my anchor confidently at daybreak, crossed the North Sea, and found that the predictions of the weather prophet were entirely correct.

On the second occasion I was crossing the Cattegat on my way to the Sound and Copenhagen. I had been sailing for a day and a night before a light breeze, with no appearances of bad weather in the sky. But the glass had fallen a quarter of an inch in the night and was still falling; so I made for the nearest port of refuge on the Zeeland coast, a little fishing-haven called Gillelie. When I sailed in I found that a *fête* was in progress, the fishermen enjoying themselves; for this happened to be the last day of their idle season; all the herringers were ready for sea, and were about to sail to the fishing-grounds round the island of Anholt on the following morning.

'I suppose you will be sailing at the same time as we do,' said a fisherman to me.

'I don't think that any of us will sail to-morrow,' I replied.

'How is that?' he asked, 'the herringers must sail.'

'It will be blowing a gale from the north-west,' I said.

'Ah, you are wrong, captain, you don't know this coast like I do.'

'I don't know anything about the coast, but come below and look at our glass.'

It had fallen another quarter of an inch and was now very low.

I was sure that a strong blow was coming. I was willing to stake my reputation on it, and, if I was wrong I would never trust in a barometer again. But my friend scouted the idea of an approaching gale, said he did not believe in glasses, and, what was more to the point, did not understand them. 'The wind is south-west,' he urged; 'we never get bad weather from that quarter.'

'Then it will shift to the north-east by and by,' I replied. 'I am sure that I at any rate, will *not* sail to-morrow.'

That night, while we were watching a firework display on a hill above the village, the wind suddenly shifted to north-west and soon a violent gale was howling through the bending pines, and the Sound beneath us became white with foam. For two days it blew a hurricane. The fishermen, far from putting to sea, were all busy securing their vessels, for there was some danger of these being dashed to pieces even in this sheltered haven. No such storm had been known for some years, and there was much loss of life and shipping on the Baltic.

This made a convert of my friend the fisherman. 'I shall believe in barometers for the future,' he said. 'It is very fortunate for us that yesterday's fête kept us all in port. Had it taken place two Sundays ago, as was originally intended, we should now have been off Anholt, where there is no harbour or shelter, and I think that many of our vessels and lives would have been lost. A few years ago a gale came on suddenly like this one, and twenty boats were capsized by the seas on the Anholt shoals, and all hands were drowned.' Mine was actually the only glass in the harbour; but the accuracy of my forecast so impressed the Gillelie fishermen that they applied to the Danish Government for one of the barometers which it supplies to seaports for the public use.

It need scarcely be pointed out that the storm signals, which are hoisted at our principal ports whenever the Meteorological Department of the Board of Trade gives the warning, must not be disregarded. Do not venture to cross the North Sea, for example, with your little craft, if any of the ominous cones or drums are shown. A cone, when hoisted base downwards, indicates the probability of a gale from the northward; an inverted cone (that is, a cone having its apex pointing downwards), of a gale from the southward; a drum, of dangerous winds from nearly opposite quarters successively; the north cone hoisted over the drum, of dangerous winds, first from the northward; the south cone hoisted underneath the drum, of dangerous winds at first from the southward; These warnings and the forecasts of the Meteorological Office published in the daily papers often give notice of coming disturbances a considerable time before one's barometer on board shows any sign, for they refer to yet far-off gales, whose approach to our coasts have been cabled from distant stations – for example, from the other side of the Atlantic.

A good many people are apparently under the impression that in order to foretell the weather by the barometer all one has to do is to see whether the glass is high or low, the former condition indicating fine weather, the latter foul; and that while a rising glass is a sign of an improvement in the weather, a falling glass shows that the weather is taking a change for the worse. It is true that these rules hold good generally; but one would soon come to grief if one relied implicitly upon them when making a long coasting voyage with a small yacht. As a matter of fact, a rising glass, though usually indicating fine weather, is, in certain circumstances, the sign of a strong gale of wind. To read the barometer's warnings accurately requires a careful study of the meteorological conditions; and every yachtsman should provide himself with one of the handbooks published on this subject.

A barometer merely measures the weight, or pressure, of the air, and shows by its rising and falling whether the pressure is increasing or diminishing. The air naturally has a tendency to flow from a region where the pressure is greater to a region where it is less, producing a wind in that direction. Consequently, if the glass stands steadily for some time at what is its average height in that portion of the globe (in England the average height of the glass, at sea-level, is about thirty inches) it is a sign that no great atmospheric changes are taking place, the pressure being evenly distributed, and that, therefore, there will be but moderate winds and settled weather. On the other hand, a considerable rise or fall (more especially the latter) of the glass, above or below the average height, indicates a great unevenness in the atmospheric pressure, and hence gales may be expected to restore the equilibrium. When the glass falls to twenty-nine inches there is a certainty of bad weather.

It is not possible to arrive at a reliable forecast with the barometer alone. In order to foretell the nature of the change of weather indicated by a moving glass, that is, in order to ascertain from which quarter the wind may be expected to come, whether it will be accompanied by rain or snow, and so forth, one must take into consideration, in conjunction with the barometer readings, the existing meteorological conditions – the temperature of the air, the amount of moisture in the air, and the direction and force of the wind blowing at the time. It is not necessary to provide oneself with an instrument for testing the amount of moisture in the air, and a hygrometer seldom forms part of the equipment of the small yacht, as good forecasts can be made without its assistance; but a thermometer must always be carried at sea to supplement the information given by one's aneroid.

In our latitudes the thermometer rises with winds from south round by south-east to east, and falls with winds from north round by north-west to west.

Air charged with vapour is lighter than dry air; and heated air, being more rarified, is lighter than cold air. It therefore follows that, other conditions remaining unchanged, either an increase of moisture or an increase of temperature will cause the barometer to fall; while drier weather, or a fall in the temperature, will cause the barometer to rise. Thus it is that the glass falls lowest with the rainy warm south-westerly winds; and rises highest with winds from the north-east, which are both cold and dry. Thus, too, if the barometer falls considerably, while the thermometer indicates a low temperature for the time of the year, the wind will probably come from a northerly direction; whereas, if the barometer is falling, with the temperature of the air high for the time of the year, southerly winds may be expected.

With the degree of moisture, the temperature of the air and the direction of the wind remaining unchanged, a fall of the glass indicates an increase of the force of the wind from the same direction.

These are Admiral Fitzroy's two general rules for barometer readings in our latitudes:

The barometer *rises* for northerly wind (including from N.W. by the N. to E.), for dry or less wet weather, for less wind, or for more than one of these changes; except on a few occasions, when rain or snow comes from the north, with strong wind.

The barometer *falls* for south wind (including from S.E. by the S. to W.), for wet weather, for stronger wind, or for more than one of these changes, except on a few occasions, when moderate wind, with rain or snow, comes from the northward.

The following are among the most important of the rules that have been laid down by meteorologists:

As the barometer is affected by the direction of the wind, the degree of moisture in the air and the force of the wind, the greatest rise or fall of the glass will occur when these act in conjunction.

The barometer is lowest for wind and rain together, as with a south-west gale, and also when a thaw succeeding a frost saturates the air with moisture.

The barometer is highest with cold and dry north-east winds, when the air is at its heaviest, and also during severe frost.

A sudden rise or fall of the barometer indicates a change in the weather that will not last long. But if the glass rises or falls steadily for several days, there will be a long continuance of whatever change of the weather is coming. As the sailors put it: 'Long foretold, long last; short warning, soon past.'

A barometer at about thirty inches, steady or rising, with temperature falling and moisture decreasing, indicates wind from the north-west round by north to north-east, or less wind. A falling barometer, with temperature rising and moisture increasing, indicates wind and rain, or snow, from the south-east round by south to the south-west.

It is important to remember that the wind usually veers with the sun – that is, in the Northern Hemisphere, from left to right. An easterly wind, for example, changes to west through S.E., S., and S.W. If it backs round the other way – that is, through N.E., N., and N.W. – this is nearly always a sign of bad weather.

In order to obtain as reliable a forecast as possible, one should compare the conclusions arrived at from one's observation of the barometer, thermometer, and hygrometer, with the warnings given by the appearance of the heavens, and other natural phenomena. If the latter corroborate the former, one may be confident that one's prognostications are pretty correct. The weather-wisdom of the mariner consists in his true reading of these signs, of which a few of the most important will now be given.

A grey sky in the morning is a sign of fine weather; a high dawn, of wind. A red sky at sunset presages fine weather; a red sky in the morning, bad weather. Soft-looking clouds foretell fine weather with moderate winds; hard-edged, oily-looking clouds, and ragged clouds, foretell wind. A bright yellow sky at sunset indicates the approach of wind; a pale yellow or a greenish sky, rain. A dark blue sky presages wind; a light blue sky, fine weather. A great clearness of the atmosphere near the horizon, with distant objects raised by reflection, signifies rain, and possibly wind. A halo round the moon, if appearing distant though distinct, indicates wind, and probably rain. Dew is. an indication of fine weather.

A phosphorescent sea at night; the presence of great numbers of jelly-fish in the water; and shoals of herrings playing on the surface, indicate a continuance of fine warm weather with light winds. When porpoises are seen gambolling close to shore, and when they ascend tidal rivers, or when sea-birds fly inland, stormy weather is to be expected.

11

Description of a Voyage

In the last chapter I have shown how, by the use of charts, lead-line, log, calculation of the tides, etc., the mariner is enabled to direct his course along the coast and find his way when out of sight of land. In the present chapter I propose to make this more clear by conducting the reader on an imaginary voyage from one port to another, across a broad channel.

Fig. 69 (p. 138) roughly represents a portion of an ordinary chart, the soundings and other numerous details which appear on a chart being omitted. We will suppose that our little vessel is lying at anchor off the port at X, in the lower left-hand corner of the chart, and that it is our object to cross to the opposite coast and sail into the estuary Z, which is to the north-east of us. We have been for some days awaiting a 'slant'; and now, at last, our barometer, the weather forecast in the papers, and the appearance of the sky indicate settled fine weather, so we decide to start. It is true that, according to the vane, the wind will be right in our teeth; but ours is a weatherly boat, the breeze is fresh and steady, and if we work our tides scientifically we ought to be able to make the passage in twelve hours.

It is early morning, the last of the ebb runningout, when we weigh our anchor. We commence our cruise with a long turn to windward down the bay. On scanning our chart we note that extensive shoals, whose edges are marked by buoys, hem in the navigable channel on either side, and that we have to keep the conical buoys on our port hand and the flat-topped on our starboard, in order to avoid running aground. So we take care not to stand on too long on either tack, but go about in time, keeping well within the warning marks; and, at last, having got clear of all dangers, we are well outside the bay, in deep water, at some distance from the land, but with the landmarks on shore still clearly visible.

Now is the time to take our departure, as it is called; that is, we will determine, before losing sight of land, our exact position, noting the time of the observation. It is from these data that we shall make our future calculations to ascertain our position, when on the open sea, with no land in sight. There are various ways of taking a departure. In the present instance we will take it by *crossbearings*. On looking back towards the coast we perceive two well-known landmarks which are indicated on our chart – the lighthouse at *A* and the church at *B*. With the compass we take the bearings of these and find that *A* bears S. by E. of us, and *B* W.S.W. Our compass has no deviation, else we should now have to correct these bearings according to the rules already explained; and as the compass design on the chart is magnetic and not true, we have no correction to make for variation. With our parallel rules we now work these bearings successively across the chart from the compass design to *A* and *B*, and from these points we draw two lines in the direction of the bearings. Where these lines cut each other, at *C*, is the exact position of our vessel at the time we took the bearings. We next measure the distance from the ship to either landmark or to our port, with the dividers, reading off the number of miles on the graduated meridian, or on the scale of miles printed on the chart.

When taking cross-bearings in this way, select such a position that the angle between them is as nearly as possible 90 degrees; for the larger or the smaller than 90 degrees the angle is, the greater will be the error in position caused by a slight error in taking a bearing.

An *azimuth* compass is a compass specially arranged for the observation of bearings. A moveable ring is fitted on the outside of the compass-bowl, having two sight-vanes exactly opposite each other. Each vane has a vertical slit in it, the slit in one being wider than that in the other, and having a horsehair stretched vertically across it. By turning the sight-vanes in the direction of the object and looking at it through both slits, a bearing can be taken with great accuracy. Azimuth compasses are not often carried on small yachts; but an ordinary steering compass can be made to serve for an azimuth by removing the cover from the binnacle and laying an improvised azimuth ring on the top of the compass-bowl. A flat brass ring with two vertical pins at opposite sides of it will answer this purpose very well. Even without this, one can take a sufficiently correct bearing by looking along a pencil or a piece of string held across the centre of the compass and directed towards the object.

Having ascertained our position, it behoves us to consider how we shall set to work to sail our boat to its destination as rapidly as possible. When sailing for a port to windward, it is the general rule to keep on that tack on which the vessel looks up best for her port – that is, the tack which makes the direction in which she is heading and the bearing of her port form the smaller angle. As soon as she has reached a position which makes the other tack the most favourable, she should be put about. By following this plan no change of wind can place the vessel in a worse position; indeed, any change will be in her favour; whereas, if one stand on long on the tack on which she looks up worse to her port, a shift of wind may put her dead to leeward of her destination, and she wiil have lost instead of having gained ground.

But in the case before us, as I have already said, the wind is right ahead – that is, from the N.E. – so that we would look up for our port equally well on either tack. However, on studying the tide-tables and the chart, we find that the flood-tide is now beginning to make, and is setting in the direction of the arrow on the chart – that is, north (magnetic). This decides us to lay our vessel on the port tack; for by doing so we *underbow* the tide, as it is called – that is, we cause it to serve us by making it set the vessel, broadside on, to windward; so that though, while sailing close-hauled, her course *through the water* is about east, she is really travelling *over the ground* in a direction considerably to the north of east – that is, much more directly for her port than she would do on the starboard tack.

So having taken our departure at C, we sail away on the port tack and soon lose sight of land. As we have a long passage before us, and we wish to cross the Channel without delay, we must sail our vessel a good full and bye – that is, we must take care not to keep her too close up to the wind, with sails ever on the shake; neither must we haul our sheets aft over much, to flatten in our sails. For if we fall into these errors we shall discover that, though our vessel points up well for her port, she has been so pinned down that she will be almost as sluggish as a craft that is hove-to; she will make but slow progress, and will drift away to leeward. More especially when there is a choppy sea on to deaden your vessel's way, keep her ramping full when on a passage.

Having sailed, let us say, for four hours from our point of departure C, and being well out of sight of land, we bethink ourselves to once more ascertain our whereabouts. We have been steering from in an east by north direction – that is, towards D. It has already been shown that even a deep-keel boat, when close-hauled, is driven away to leeward, so that her real direction through the water is at an angle with the direction in which she is heading; and that a vessel will make greater leeway if the sea be rough. It is easy to measure the amount of leeway by looking over the stern and observing the vessel's wake – that is, the track she leaves behind her in the water; the angle the wake makes with the keel being the angle of leeway. We will suppose that this angle, in the present case, is about one point of the compass. Then our course through the water has been one point to leeward of east by north – that is, it has been east (magnetic), in the direction C E, which we now lay down with our parallel rulers on the chart. Next we calculate (having hove the log occasionally, or having made a rough estimate by looking over the side) how many miles we have travelled *through the water* since we left the point C, and with the dividers we measure out this distance from the scale of miles on the chart, and lay it down from C on the line of our course, making C E equal to the distance. E would then be our present position, had no current been running since our start.

But when we left C the flood-tide was just beginning to make, and has been setting us in a northerly direction for four hours. On reference to the arrow on the chart, we find that at half-flood the rate of the tide is six miles an hour. In the last chapter I have explained that in the open sea at half-flood the tide is at its strongest, rising then as much in one hour as it does in the first two hours of the flood. From this we can therefore calculate that the drift of the flood has been about eighteen miles during the four hours since we took our departure. From E we draw on the chart a line parallel to the arrow which indicates the direction of the current, and with the dividers we measure out upon it, from the scale of miles on the chart, E F equal to eighteen miles. Then F is our true position, and C F is the distance we have made. What we have gained by putting our vessel on the port tack, and so underbowing the tide, now becomes very apparent; for our true course has been north-easterly, that is, we have travelled over the ground right in the teeth of the wind and directly for our destination, being now about half-way to it; whereas, had we laid the yacht on the starboard tack, we should in the same time have only reached the point Y.

Supposing that the wind had been favourable for our port when we left C, we should have employed the following method of ascertaining the course to be steered so as to make allowance for current. Let L in the diagram, at the foot of Fig. 69, represent the vessel's point of departure, and let P be her destination. With the dividers we take from the scale of miles the number of miles the current runs in one hour, and lay this distance down from L to N, making L N parallel to the direction of the current. Then we take the number of miles which we estimate the vessel will sail in one hour, and with this distance as a radius and A as a centre describe a circle. We join M, the point where this circle cuts the line L P, with N; and from L we draw L O equal and parallel to N M. L O is the direction in which we must steer to keep the vessel on the line *L P,* and also represents the distance that must be sailed in order to reach *M.*

In the above example, the current affects the ship's course as well as her rate of progress over the ground. If the current's drift is in the same direction as the ship's apparent course there is no alteration of her course, but the distance travelled will be the sum of the distance logged and the number of miles of the current's drift; and if the two are in opposite directions, it will be the difference between these. Thus, had we sailed from *C* on the starboard tack, we should have travelled over the ground in the direction we were heading – that is, north; and *C Y,* the distance we should have made, would have been equal to *C E* plus *E F.*

I have taken it for granted, in this description of our proceedings, that the flood-tide preserves a uniform northerly set. This, by the way, is unlikely to be the case. In the open sea the tide, as a rule, runs in different directions at different hours of the flood – for example, setting north at half-flood and north-east at the fourth hour, – and this difference of direction, if considerable, must be taken into account.

Having ascertained our position at *F,* we decide to keep the vessel on the same tack; not only because the flood is still making, and we can continue to underbow the tide, but also because it will be advisable to get hold of the land before the tide turns; then, in case the wind falls light, we can anchor until the next flood, and not lose the ground we have made. We know that the flood-stream is already slacking; consequently we must not expect to do quite so well as we have so far done; our true course will no longer be north-east, straight for our port, but will be a good deal to the eastward of this.

The wind holds, and at last we sight the opposite coast, sail on until we are a few miles off the shore, and recognise a landmark, the tower *G,* over our starboard bow; so we have made a landfall, as we expected we should do, considerably to the southward of the estuary for which we are bound. Our tide-tables show us that it is now high-water, and that we shall shortly have the ebb-stream setting to the south dead against us. It is important to remember, by the way, that the time of high-water is very rarely the time at which the stream alters its direction. As a rule, the flood-stream runs for a considerable time after high-water, while the ebb-stream likewise often runs long after the tide has commenced to rise. But on this occasion we satisfy ourselves that the flood-stream has quite spent itself at the spot where we are; for when we look carefully at a tree or some other object which is directly ahead of us on the shore, we observe that it does not alter its bearings as we near it, or only does so to an extent that our leeway will account for. It follows, therefore, that our vessel is not being affected by any current, and that it is slack water.

After studying the conditions we decide to stand in as near as we safely can, and then to go about.

By doing this we will cheat the ebb-stream when it begins to make itself felt; for we know that hereabouts the tides, as is often the case, do not run nearly so rapidly in the shoal-water under the land as they do outside. Moreover, a look at the chart shows us that we shall be able on the starboard tack to fetch the mouth of our river without having to go about again and so lose ground by bringing the contrary current broadside on to us.

But our chart indicates submerged rocky patches, which make it perilous to approach within a certain distance of the shore, so we must now take crossbearings again to ascertain our position, and enable us to give these dangers a sufficiently wide berth. We took our departure at C by cross-bearings of two well-known landmarks, which is the most accurate method: but it happens that on this portion of the coast there are no two landmarks whose positions are shown on the chart; we must, therefore, adopt another method.

If we take a bearing of an object, sail for a known distance in a known direction, and then take another bearing of it, the distance we have made and the two bearings form a triangle of which we know the value of the angles, and of one of the sides;

consequently by constructing this triangle on a sheet of paper we can easily estimate the length of the other sides and our distance from the object. The simplest method of finding one's position by taking two bearings of the same object is the one we shall adopt in the present instance. In the first place, having stood on as far as we prudently can on the port tack, we go about, and find that our vessel on the starboard tack heads up due north, sailing parallel to the coast. We now take a bearing of some object on the shore, selecting one that is over our bows and not abreast or astern of us. In this case the tower G will answer our purpose very well. We observe the angle that this bearing makes with our course, and we sail on until this angle is doubled; then the number of miles we have sailed since taking the first bearing is our present distance from G. Thus, when we tack ship at K, we find that G bears north-east of us, and therefore G K H, the angle between this bearing and the northerly course we now pursue, equals four points of the compass, or 45 degrees. We sail on to H when G bears due east of us, so that G H Z, the angle between the bearing and our course, has doubled, being eight points, or 90 degrees. Consequently, as any schoolboy can explain to us from his Euclid, the line H K is equal to H G – that is, our present distance from G is the number of miles we have made while sailing from K to H, allowance having, of course, been made for the set and drift of the current.

As a rule, cross-bearings taken in this way are not nearly so reliable as those taken of two objects from one position, in the manner already explained; for unless we have an accurate knowledge of the local currents, we can only approximately calculate the true distance and course made by the vessel in the interval between taking the two bearings. But in the present case, as we happen to be sailing slowly and are in shallow water, we are enabled by employing what is termed the ground-log to gauge with great precision the effect of any stream that may be running, and to lay down our exact position on the chart. To effect this we attach our ordinary log-line to our hand-lead and heave it over the stern. We then reel out the line and employ the log-glass just as we would do when heaving the log-ship; but the lead, instead of being suspended in the water, as is the log-ship during the operation, remains fixed on the bottom; and therefore, when we read off the knots we are making, we ascertain not our rate through the water, as is the case when we employ the log-ship, but our speed over the ground. The direction in which the line leads over the stern indicates the direction in which we are moving over the ground, forming an angle with our keel if the current is not exactly with or against us, or if we are making leeway.

Having now reached the position *H,* and having satisfied ourselves, after a glance at the chart, that there are no more rocky patches ahead to pick us up, we sail on as near to the wind as we can without pinning the vessel down too much, and edge in towards the shore, so as to avoid the strength of the ebb stream, which is now running south. At last we enter the estuary, and as current and wind are both unfavourable for the ascent of the river, we are compelled to come to an anchor and wait the turn of the tide.

We should probably have acted thus had the wind been fair, for we are not familiar with the somewhat dangerous mouth of this river, though we know that its channel winds among great shoals which are but badly marked with occasional poles. At this stage of the tide (the ebb, we will suppose, has been running for two hours) all these shoals are still covered and the channel is difficult to find, so that if we endeavour to sail up we shall most probably run ashore before we get far, and be left high and dry amid the mud-banks by the receding tide – always an undignified position. On the other hand, if we remain at anchor until low water, we can easily, without running the risk of getting stuck in the mud for hours, pick our way up the river on the beginning of the flood; for then the shoals are uncovered, and the channels between them are clearly defined. We cannot well miss our way, and even if we do run aground, the rising tide will soon float us *off.*

I have taken it for granted that we have had fine weather during our voyage, for the management of a small yacht in heavy weather is a subject that has already been dealt with in another chapter. But there is one matter to which I should like to make reference here. If there is a good harbour under our lee we should of course, as a rule, run for it when overtaken by a gale; but if we are off a dangerous coast, with only small and difficult harbours or river-mouths under our lee, with which we are not acquainted, whose leading marks do not appear on our chart, and into which it would be hazardous to try to find our way without a pilot, it is often the more prudent course not to seek shelter, but to ride out the gale on the open sea as one best can, hove-to under storm canvas or riding to a deep-sea anchor. I was once cruising with a friend who was a fairly good fore-and-aft sailor, but who got scared on one occasion when we were on a lee-shore and it came on to blow hard. He was anxious to run blindly for the mouth of a narrow river obstructed by a dangerous and often-shifting bar (on which the sea was breaking heavily at the time), with the passage across which neither of us was acquainted. He called this prudence, but it was in truth the rashness of panic. I knew that we should in all probability lose our vessel if we made the attempt he proposed, and I insisted on keeping to the open sea. We close-reefed our little vessel, and, facing the gale, put her at it, got a good offing by sailing for some distance on the tack which took her best away from the land, and then hove her to. She rode the gale out beautifully, and next morning my friend had to confess that mine had been the most prudent plan after all. But safer still is it, when cruising with a small craft, to do as I have already recommended, that is, to so watch the weather forecasts and the glass, that one never allows oneself to be surprised by a strong gale when at a long distance from a secure harbour.

12

Board of Trade and Other Regulations Affecting Yachtsmen

He who undertakes to command even the smallest craft should thoroughly master the rules of the road at sea, else he will soon find himself in difficulties, and will endanger the lives and property of himself and others. Knowledge of the law is presumed; ignorance of it is no defence; and any one who unwittingly infringes one of the Board of Trade regulations is liable to a penalty of £20, even if the infringement has caused no damage.

The Admiralty and Board of Trade have recently framed revised regulations for preventing collisions at sea; these differ in several important respects from the old rules, and came into force on July 1, 1897. The yachtsman, as master of a sailing vessel, is concerned not only with the rules (as to carrying lights, etc.) to be observed by himself, but also with the rules applying to steamers, tugs, towing-vessels, fishing-boats, and disabled craft; for he must be familiar with these in order that he may understand the signals and movements of the vessels and so avoid collision. It is unnecessary in a work of this description to compare the new regulations with the old. That has been admirably done, by the way, from the legal point of view as well as from the sailor's, by Mr H. Stewart Moore in his work on the subject published by J. D. Potter.

The following are the new regulations:

PRELIMINARY

These rules shall be followed by all vessels upon the high seas and in all waters connected therewith, navigable by sea-going vessels.

In the following rules every steam vessel which is under sail and not under steam is to be considered a sailing vessel, and every vessel under steam, whether under sail or not, is to be considered a steam vessel.

The word 'steam vessel' shall include any vessel propelled by machinery (e.g. electric launches).

A vessel is 'under way' within the meaning of these rules, when she is not at anchor, or made fast to the shore, or aground.

RULES CONCERNING LIGHTS, ETC.

The word 'visible' in these rules, when applied to lights, shall mean visible on a dark night with a clear atmosphere.

Art. 1. The rules concerning lights shall be complied with in all weathers from sunset to sunrise, and during such time no other lights which may be mistaken for the prescribed lights shall be exhibited.

Art. 2. A steam vessel when under way shall carry:

(a) On, or in front of the foremast, or if a vessel without a foremast then in the fore part of the vessel, at a height above the hull of not less than 20 feet, and if the breadth of the vessel exceeds 20 feet, then at a height above the hull not less than such breadth, so, however, that the light need not be carried at a greater height above the hull' than 40 feet, a bright white light, so constructed as to show an unbroken light over an arc of the horizon of 20 points of the compass, so fixed as to throw the light 10 points on each side of the vessel, viz. from right ahead to two points abaft the beam on either side, and of such a character as to be visible at a distance of at least five miles.

(b) On the starboard side a green light so constructed as to show an unbroken light over an arc of the horizon of 10 points of the compass, so fixed as to throw the light from right ahead to two points abaft the beam on the starboard side, and of such a character as to be visible at a distance of at least two miles.

(c) On the port side a red light so constructed as to show an unbroken light over an arc of the horizon of 10 points of the compass, so fixed as to throw the light from right ahead to two

points abaft the beam on the port side, and of such a character as to be visible at a distance of at least two miles.

(d)   The said green and red side-lights shall be fitted with inboard screens projecting at least three feet forward from the light, so as to prevent these lights from being seen across the bow.

(e)   A steam vessel when under way may carry an additional white light similar in construction to the light mentioned in subdivision *(a)*. These two lights shall be so placed in line with the keel that one shall be at least 15 feet higher than the other, and in such a position with reference to each other that the lower light shall be forward of the upper one. The vertical distance between these lights shall be less than the horizontal distance.

Art. 3. A steam vessel when towing another vessel shall, in addition to her side-lights, carry two bright white lights in a vertical line one over the other, not less than six feet apart, and when towing more than one vessel shall carry an additional bright white light six feet above or below such lights, if the length of the tow, measuring from the stern of the towing vessel to the stern of the last vessel towed, exceeds 600 feet. Each of these lights shall be of the same construction and character, and shall be carried in the same position, as the white light mentioned in **Art. 2.** *(a)*, except the additional light, which may be carried at a height of not less than 14 feet above the hull.

Such steam vessel may carry a small white light abaft the funnel or aftermast for the vessel towed to steer by, but such light shall not be visible forward of the beam.

Art. 4. *(a)* A vessel which from any accident is not under command shall carry, at the same height as the white light mentioned in **Art. 2.** *(a)* where they can best be seen (and, if a steam vessel, in lieu of that light), two red lights, in a vertical line one over the other, not less than six feet apart, and of such a character as to be visible all round the horizon at a distance of at least two miles; and shall by day carry in a vertical line one over the other, not less than six feet apart, where they can best be seen, two black balls or shapes each two feet in diameter.

(b) A vessel employed in laying or in picking up a telegraph cable shall carry in the same position as the white light mentioned in **Art. 2.** *(a)*, (and, if a steam vessel, in lieu of that light), three lights in a vertical line one over the other, not less than six feet apart. The highest and lowest of these lights shall be red, and the middle light shall be white, and they shall be of such a character as to be visible all round the horizon at a distance of at least two miles. By day she shall carry in a vertical line one over the other, not less than six feet apart, where they can best be seen, three shapes not less than two feet in diameter, of which the highest and lowest shall be globular in shape and red in colour, and the middle one diamond in shape and white.

(c) The vessels referred to in this Article, when not making way through the water, shall not carry the sidelights, but when making way shall carry them.

(d) The lights and shapes required to be shown by this Article are to be taken by other vessels as signals that the vessel showing them is not under command, and cannot therefore get out of the way.

These signals are not signals of vessels in distress and requiring assistance. Such signals are contained in **Art. 31**.

Art. 5. A sailing vessel under way, and any vessel being towed, shall carry the same lights as are prescribed by **Art. 2.** for a steam vessel under way, with the exception of the white lights mentioned therein, which they shall never carry.

Art. 6. Whenever, as in the case of small vessels under way during bad weather, the green and red side-lights cannot be fixed, these lights shall be kept at hand lighted and ready for use; and shall, on the approach of or to other vessels, be exhibited on their respective sides in sufficient time to prevent collision, in such manner as to make them most visible, and so that the green light shall not be seen on the port side nor the red light on the starboard side, nor, if practicable, more than two points abaft the beam on their respective sides.

To make the use of these portable lights more certain and easy, the lanterns containing them shall each be painted outside with the colour of the light they respectively contain, and shall be provided with proper screens.

Art. 7. Steam vessels of less than 40, and vessels under oars or sails of less than 20, tons gross tonnage respectively, and rowing boats, when under way, shall not be obliged to carry the lights mentioned in Art. 2. *(a)*, *(b)*, and *(c)*, but if they do not carry them they shall be provided with the following lights:

1.   Steam vessels of less than 40 tons shall carry:

(a)   In the fore part of the vessel, or on or in front of the funnel, where it can best be seen, and at a height above the gunwale of not less than nine feet, a bright white light constructed and fixed as prescribed in Art. 2. *(a)*, and of such a character as to be visible at a distance of at least two miles.

(b)   Green and red side-lights constructed and fixed as prescribed in Art. 2. *(b)* and *(c)*, and of such a character as to be visible at a distance of at least one mile, or a combined lantern showing a green light and a red light from right ahead to two points abaft the beam on their respective sides. Such lantern shall be carried not less than three feet below the white light.

2.   Small steamboats, such as are carried by sea-going vessels, may carry the white light at a less height than nine feet above the gunwale, but it shall be carried above the combined lantern mentioned in subdivision 1. *(b)*.

3.   Vessels under oars or sails, of less than 20 tons, shall have ready at hand a lantern with a green glass on one side and a red glass on the other, which, on the approach of or to other vessels, shall be exhibited in sufficient time to prevent collision, so that the green light shall not be seen on the port side nor the red light on the starboard side.

4.   Rowing boats, whether under oars or sails, shall have ready at hand a lantern, showing a white light, which shall be temporarily exhibited in sufficient time to prevent collision. The vessels referred to in this Article shall not be obliged to carry the lights prescribed by Art. 4. *(a)* and Art. 11., last paragraph.

Art. 8. Pilot vessels, when engaged on their station on pilotage duty, shall not show the lights required for other vessels, but shall carry a white light at the masthead, visible all round the horizon, and shall also exhibit a flare-up light or flare-up lights at short intervals, which shall never exceed 15 minutes.

On the near approach of or to other vessels they shall have their side-lights lighted, ready for use, and shall flash or show them at short intervals, to indicate the direction in which they are heading; but the green light shall not be shown on the port side, nor the red light on the starboard side.

A pilot vessel of such a class as to be obliged to go alongside of a vessel to put a pilot on board, may show the white light instead of carrying it at the masthead, and may, instead of the coloured lights above mentioned, have at hand, ready for use, a lantern with a green glass on the one side and a red glass on the other, to be used as prescribed above.

Pilot vessels, when not engaged on their station on pilotage duty, shall carry lights similar to those of other vessels of their tonnage.

Art. 9. This Article, which will deal with the regulations affecting fishing-boats, will be the subject of a future Order in Council. For the present, the corresponding Article (**Art. 10**) of the old rules remains in force. It applies only to fishing vessels and boats when in the sea, off the coast of Europe lying north of Cape Finisterre. The following is a summary of its regulations:

(a)   All fishing-boats of 20 tons net registered tonnage or upwards, when under way, and when not required by the following regulations in this Article to carry and show the lights therein named, shall carry and show the same lights as other vessels under way.

(b) and *(c)* All vessels when engaged with drift-nets, or employed in line-fishing with their lines out, shall exhibit two white lights, placed so that the vertical distance between them shall be not less than six feet and not more than ten feet, and so that the horizontal distance between them shall be not less than five feet and not more than ten feet. The lower of these two lights shall be the more forward, and both of them shall be of such a character, and contained in lanterns of such construction, as to show all

round the horizon on a dark night, with a clear atmosphere, for a distance of not more than three miles.

(*d*) If a vessel, when fishing, becomes stationary, in consequence of her gear getting fast to a rock or other obstruction, she shall show the light and make the fog-signal for a vessel at anchor.

(*e*) Fishing-vessels, when trawling, dredging, or fishing with any kind of drag-net, may use a flare-up in addition to the lights prescribed by this Article; the flare-up to be shown at the after-part of the vessel, excepting that, if the vessel be hanging by the stern to her trawl, dredge, or drag-net, it shall be exhibited from her bow.

(*f*) In fog, mist, or falling snow, a vessel engaged in fishing with trawl-nets, lines, etc., shall, at intervals of not more than two minutes, make a blast with her fog-horn and ring her bell alternately.

The following regulations were added by subsequent Orders in Council:

A British steam trawler of 20 tons register or upwards under steam, with trawl in the water, and not being stationary for reasons specified in subdivision (*d*), shall, between sunset and sunrise, either carry and show the lights required by **Art. 2.**, or shall carry and show in lieu thereof, but not in addition thereto, other lights of the description set forth below:

On or in front of the foremast head, and in the same position as the white light which other steamships are required to carry, a lanthorn showing a white light ahead, a green light on the starboard side, and a red light on the port side; such lanthorn to be so fixed as to show the white light from right ahead to two points on the bow on each side of the ship, the green light from two points on the starboard bow to four points abaft the beam on the starboard side, and the red light from two points on the port bow to four points abaft the beam on the port side; and (**2**) a white light in a globular lanthorn so constructed as to show a light all round the horizon; this lanthorn to be carried lower than the lanthorn showing the white, red, and green lights as aforesaid, so, however, that the vertical distance between them shall not be less than six feet nor more than twelve feet.

British sailing trawlers of 20 tons register or upwards, having their trawls in the water and not being stationary, shall carry and show the lights required by **Art. 5.**, or shall carry and show in lieu thereof, but not in addition thereto, the following lights: On or in front of the foremast-head a lanthorn having a green glass on the starboard side, and a red glass on the port side, so arranged that the red and green do not converge, and so as to show the green light from the right ahead to four points abaft the beam on the starboard side, and the red light from right ahead to four points abaft the beam on the port side; and (2) a white light in a globular lanthorn similar to that mentioned in the last paragraph as carried by the steam trawler, and similarly situated.

Or a white light in a globular lanthorn so constructed as to show a light all around the horizon, and visible on a dark night, with a clear atmosphere, for a distance of at least two miles; and also a sufficient supply of red pyrotechnic lights, which shall each bum for at least thirty seconds, and shall, when so burning, be visible for the same distance under the same conditions as the white light. The white light shall be shown from sunset to sunrise, and one of the red pyrotechnic lights shall be shown on approaching, or on being approached by, another vessel in sufficient time to prevent collision.

Art. 10. A vessel which is being overtaken by another shall show from her stern to such last-mentioned vessel a white light or a flare-up light.

The white light required to be shown by this Article may be fixed and carried in a lantern, but in such case the lantern shall be so constructed, fitted, and screened that it shall throw an unbroken light over an arc of the horizon of twelve points of the compass, viz. from six points from right aft on each side of the vessel, so as to be visible at a distance of at least one mile. Such light shall be carried as nearly as practicable on the same level as the side-lights.

Art. 11. A vessel under 150 feet in length, when at anchor, shall carry forward where it can best be seen, but at a height not exceeding 20 feet above the hull, a white light in a lantern so constructed as to show a clear, uniform, and unbroken light, visible all round the horizon at the distance of at least one mile.

A vessel of 150 feet or upwards in length, when at anchor, shall carry in the forward part of the vessel, at a height of not less than 20, and not exceeding 40, feet above the hull, one such light, and at or near the stern of the vessel, and at such a height that it shall be not less than 15 feet lower than the forward light, another such light.

The length of a vessel shall be deemed to be the length appearing in her certificate of registry.

A vessel aground in or near a fairway shall carry the above light or lights, and the two red lights prescribed by Article 4 *(a)*.

Art. 12. Every vessel may, if necessary, in order to attract attention, in addition to the lights which she is by these rules required to carry, show a flare-up light, or use any detonating signal that cannot be mistaken for a distress signal.

Art. 13. Nothing in these rules shall interfere with the operation of any special rules made by the Government of any nation with respect to additional station and signal lights for two or more ships of war, or for vessels sailing under convoy, or with the exhibition of recognition signals adopted by shipowners, which have been authorised by their respective Governments, and duly registered and published.

Art. 14. A steam vessel proceeding under sail only, but having her funnel up, shall carry in daytime, forward, where it can best be seen, one black ball or shape two feet in diameter.

SOUND SIGNALS FOR FOG, ETC.

Art. 15. All signals prescribed by this Article for vessels under way shall be given:

1.   By 'steam vessels' on the whistle or siren.
2.   By 'sailing vessels and vessels towed' on the foghorn. The

words 'prolonged blast' used in this Article shall mean a blast of from four to six minutes' duration.

A steam vessel shall be provided with an efficient whistle or siren, sounded by steam or some substitute for steam, so placed that the sound may not be intercepted by any obstruction, and with an efficient fog-horn, to be sounded by mechanical means, and also with an efficient bell. A sailing vessel of 20 tons gross tonnage or upwards shall be provided with a similar fog-horn and bell.

In fog, mist, falling snow, or heavy rain-storms, whether by day or night, the signals described in this Article shall be used as follows, viz.:

(a)   A steam vessel having way upon her shall sound, at intervals of not more than two minutes, a prolonged blast.

(b)   A steam vessel under way, but stopped and having no way upon her, shall sound, at intervals of not more than two minutes, two prolonged blasts, with an interval of about one second between them.

(c)   A sailing vessel under way shall sound, at intervals of not more than one minute, when on the starboard tack one blast, when on the port tack two blasts in succession, and when with the wind abaft the beam three blasts in succession.

(d)   A vessel, when at anchor, shall, at intervals of not more than one minute, ring the bell rapidly for about five seconds.

(e)   A vessel when towing, a vessel employed in laying or picking up a telegraph cable, and a vessel under way, which is unable to get out of the way of an approaching vessel through being not under command, or unable to manoeuvre as required by these rules, shall, instead of the signals prescribed in subdivisions *(a)* and *(c)* of this Article, at intervals of not more than two minutes sound three blasts in succession, viz. one prolonged blast followed by two short blasts. A vessel towed may give this signal, and she shall not give any other.

Sailing vessels and boats of less than 20 tons gross tonnage shall not be obliged to give the above-mentioned signals, but if they do not, they shall make some other efficient sound signal at intervals of not more than one minute.

SPEED OF SHIPS TO BE MODERATE IN FOG, ETC.

Art 16. Every vessel shall, in a fog, mist, falling snow, or heavy rain-storms, go at a moderate speed, having careful regard to the existing circumstances and conditions.

A steam vessel hearing, apparently forward of her beam, the fog-signal of a vessel the position of which is not ascertained, shall, so far as the circumstances of the case admit, stop her engines, and then navigate with caution until danger of collision is over.

PRELIMINARY – RISKS OF COLLISION

Risk of collision can, when circumstances permit, be ascertained by carefully watching the compass-bearing of an approaching vessel. If the bearing does not appreciably change, such risk should be deemed to exist.

Art 17. When two sailing vessels are approaching one another, so as to involve risk of collision, one of them shall keep out of the way of the other as follows, viz.: –

(a) A vessel which is running free shall keep out of the way of a vessel which is close-hauled.

(b) A vessel which is close-hauled on the port tack shall keep out of the way of a vessel which is close-hauled on the starboard tack.

(c) When both are running free, with the wind on different sides, the vessel which has the wind on the port side shall keep out of the way of the other.

(d) When both are running free, with the wind on the same side, the vessel which is to windward shall keep out of the way of the vessel which is to leeward.

(e) A vessel which has the wind aft shall keep out of the way of the other vessel.

Art 18. When two steam vessels are meeting end on, or nearly end on, so as to involve risk of collision, each shall alter her course to starboard, so that each may pass on the port side of the other.

This Article does not apply to two vessels which must, if both keep on their respective courses, pass clear of each other.

The only cases to which it does apply are when each of the two vessels is end on, or nearly end on, to the other: in other words, to cases in which, by day, each vessel sees the masts of the other in a line, or nearly in a line with her own; and by night, to cases in which each vessel is in such a position as to see both the side-lights of the other.

It does not apply, by day, to cases in which a vessel sees another ahead crossing her own course; or by night, to cases where the red light of one vessel is opposed to the red light of the other, or where the green light of one vessel is opposed to the green light of the other, or where a red light without a green light, or a green light without a red light, is seen ahead, or where both green and red lights are seen anywhere but ahead.

Art 19. When two steam vessels are crossing, so as to involve risk of collision, the vessel which has the other on her own starboard side shall keep out of the way of the other.

Art 20. When a steam vessel and a sailing vessel are proceeding in such directions as to involve risk of collision, the steam vessel shall keep out of the way of the sailing vessel.

Art 21. Where by any of these rules one of two vessels is to keep out of the way, the other shall keep her course and speed.

Note: When, in consequence of thick weather or other causes, such vessel finds herself so close that collision cannot be avoided by the action of the giving-way vessel alone, she also shall take such action as will best aid to avert collision.

Art 22. Every vessel which is directed by these rules to keep out of the way of another vessel shall, if the circumstances of the case admit, avoid crossing ahead of the other.

Art 23. Every steamer which is directed by these rules to keep out of the way of another vessel shall, on approaching her, if necessary, slacken her speed or stop or reverse.

Art 24. Notwithstanding anything contained in these rules, every vessel, overtaking any other, shall keep out of the way of the overtaken vessel.

Every vessel coming up with another vessel from any direction more than two points abaft her beam, i.e. in such a position, with reference to the vessel which she is overtaking, that at night she would be unable to see either of that vessel's side-lights, shall be deemed to be an overtaking vessel; and no subsequent alteration of the bearing between the two vessels shall make the overtaking vessel a crossing vessel within the meaning of these rules, or relieve her of the duty of keeping clear of the overtaking vessel until she is finally past and clear.

As by day the overtaking vessel cannot always know with certainty whether she is forward of or abaft this direction from the other vessel, she should, if in doubt, assume that she is an overtaking vessel and keep out of the way.

Art 25. In narrow channels every steam vessel shall, when it is safe and practicable, keep to that side of the fairway or mid-channel which lies on the starboard side of such vessel.

Art 26. Sailing vessels under way shall keep out of the way of sailing vessels or boats fishing with nets, or lines, or trawls. This rule shall not give to any vessel or boat engaged in fishing the right of obstructing a fairway used by vessels other than fishing vessels or boats.

Art 27. In obeying and construing these rules, due regard shall be had to all dangers of navigation and collision, and to any special circumstances which may render a departure from the above rules necessary in order to avoid immediate danger.

SOUND SIGNALS FOR VESSELS IN SIGHT OF ONE ANOTHER

Art 28. The words 'short blast used in this Article shall mean a blast of about one second's duration.

When vessels are in sight of one another, a steam vessel under way in taking any course authorised or required by these rules, shall indicate that course by the following signals on her whistle or siren, viz.:

One short blast to mean, 'I am directing my course to starboard.'

Two short blasts to mean, 'I am directing my course to port.'

Three short blasts to mean, 'My engines are full speed astern.'

NO VESSEL UNDER ANY CIRCUMSTANCES TO NEGLECT PROPER PRECAUTIONS

Art 29. Nothing in these rules shall exonerate any vessel, or the owner, or master, or crew thereof, from the consequences of any neglect to carry lights or signals, or of any neglect to keep a proper look-out, or of the neglect of any precaution which *may* be required by the ordinary practice of seamen, or by the special circumstances of the case.

RESERVATION OF RULES FOR HARBOURS AND INLAND NAVIGATION

Art 30. Nothing in these rules shall interfere with the operation of a special rule, duly made by local authority, relative to the navigation of any harbour, river, or inland waters.

DISTRESS SIGNALS

Art 31. When a vessel is in distress and requires assistance from other vessels or from the shore, the following shall be the signals to be used or displayed by her, either together or separately, viz.:

In the daytime:

1. A gun or other explosive signal fired at intervals of about a minute.

2. The International Code signal of distress indicated by N.C.

3. The distant signal, consisting of a square flag, having either above or below it a ball or anything resembling a ball.

4. A continuous sounding with any fog-signal apparatus.

At night:

1. A gun or other explosive signal fired at intervals of about a minute.

2. Flames on the vessel (as from a burning tar-barrel, oil-barrel, etc.).

3. Rockets or shells, throwing stars of any colour or description, fired one at a time, at short intervals.

4. A continuous sounding with any fog-signal apparatus.

The skipper of the small yacht will discover, from a perusal of these regulations, that it is his duty to carry with him the following lanterns – a white riding light, a red port light, a green starboard light, and a white bull's-eye lantern; for he will find the bull's-eye the most convenient form of light to show from the stern when overtaken by a vessel (see **Article 10.**). The author on his cruising yachts invariably kept a lit bull's-eye lantern hanging at the top of the companion lantern at night, within easy reach of the man at the helm.

A vessel under 20 tons need not carry two sidelights, as she is permitted by Article 7 to carry a lantern with a green glass on one side and a red glass on the other, to be exhibited on the approach of a vessel. A lantern is also sold which combines in itself the port, starboard, and riding lights.

When employed in the latter capacity the coloured glasses are removed. In the case of rowing boats, even when under canvas, side-lights are not obligatory (see Article 7, subdivision 4).

It is laid down in Article 15 that a vessel of 20 tons and over must be provided with bell and mechanical fog-horn to sound signals in thick weather. For small yachts the ordinary fog-horn sounded with the mouth is all that is needed, as (see last paragraph of Article 15) no special form of sound signals are obligatory for vessels under 20 tons.

The flags of the international code of signals, with the code-book, are not obligatory, but should be carried on every yacht that undertakes long cruises.

The rules of the road are now clearly defined in the new regulations; but the skipper of the small boat must bear in mind that his craft is handier and quicker to turn than a large steamer or sailing vessel, that in narrow channels, as in the Thames, there is but little room for them and plenty for him, all the more so that with his tiny craft he can safely sail over the shoal water on either side of the buoyed channels. Thus he will rightly be expected to keep out of the way of the large craft, and he must not make himself a nuisance by sailing across the bows of an ocean steamer (for example, in Greenwich reach), relying on the rule of the road that gives his, as a sailing vessel, the right of way. There must be a give and take when applying these rules of the sea-road, as there is on land between the wheel traffic and the pedestrians in a crowded street. It is the duty of the small-boat skipper to avoid getting in the way of the big unwieldy vessels; but in order to do this let him take care to alter his course in good time, and so apprise the other vessel of his intention. If you stand on until you are just under a steamer's bows before you go about, her pilot, unaware that it is your intention to tack, may alter her course so as to pass under your stern, in which case a collision will probably ensue for which you will be entirely responsible.

In short, common sense must be employed in the application of the rules, and Article 27 practically lays down that they must be construed in accordance with their spirit and not the strict letter, and that under certain circumstances the vessel having the right, according to the rules, to stand on her course, must give way to the other vessel in order to avoid collision. Remember, for example, when observing the course of an approaching vessel, that the winding narrow channel of the river may necessitate her changing her course the next moment. Here is a case in which, when calculating what you ought to do yourself, the hard and fast rule cannot apply, as it would on the open sea, where a vessel suddenly altering her course in this way would put herself in the wrong if there was a collision.

By an order which came into force in 1898, regulating the navigation of Southampton Water, all sailing vessels must give way to steamers of 1,000 tons or over. On the Thames and Mersey there has for some time existed an unwritten law to the same effect, which it is expected will shortly receive the sanction of the legislation.

The following are the Board of Trade regulations relating to pilot signals:

IN THE DAYTIME: The following signals, numbered 1 and 2, when used or displayed together or separately, shall be deemed to be signals for a pilot in the daytime:

1.   To be hoisted at the fore, the jack or other national colour usually worn by merchant ships, having round it a white border, one-fifth of the breadth of the flag; or

2.   The international code pilotage signal, indicated by P.T.

AT NIGHT: The following signals, numbered 1 and 2, when used or displayed together or separately, shall be deemed to be signals for a pilot at night:

1.   The pyrotechnic light, commonly known as a blue light, every fifteen minutes; or

2.   A bright white light, flashed or shown at short or frequent intervals, just above the bulwarks, for about a minute at a time.

And 'Any master of a vessel who uses or displays, or causes or permits any person under his authority to use or display, any of the said signals for any other purpose than that of summoning a pilot, or uses, or causes, or permits any person under his authority to use, any other signal for a pilot, shall incur a penalty not exceeding twenty pounds.'

There are some other Board of Trade regulations with which the yachtsman should be conversant. For example, if he has sailed across the Channel to a foreign port he must report himself and get his vessel cleared at the first British port at which he calls on his return; and until this formality has been observed he must fly his ensign by day and carry a light under his bowsprit by night. Some years ago the author, ignorant of the regulation which compels all vessels from foreign ports to bring up off Gravesend for clearance before proceeding up the Thames, sailed by that place on his way from Ostend and did not let go his anchor till he was off North Woolwich pier. Here he was boarded by the Custom House officers; his name and address were taken down, and his vessel was searched. A few days later he received an ominous official document calling upon him to show cause why he should not be made to pay a certain heavy penalty for his infringement of the river Customs regulations. He pleaded ignorance, and as the authorities were satisfied that he was not on smuggling bent, the penalty on this occasion was not enforced.

SHIP'S PAPERS

An Admiralty warrant has been granted to certain of the Royal Yacht Clubs, the Royal Thames Yacht Club having been the first to receive this honour in 1835. The warrant authorises the member of one of these clubs to fly on his vessel the blue ensign of Her Majesty's fleet, and in the case of one club, the Royal Squadron, to fly the white ensign. The blue ensigns of some of these clubs also bear the distinguishing marks of the clubs – such as a crown in the centre.

The owner of a yacht, having made application through the secretary of his club, receives from the Admiralty a warrant entitling him to fly the ensign on that particular vessel, so long as she remains his property. The warrant must be returned to the Admiralty if the vessel is sold; an owner requires a separate warrant for each of his vessels, and separate warrants to fly the colours of each club to which he may belong. If a yacht owner fly such colours without having obtained a warrant, he will be liable to pay a penalty not exceeding £500, according to the provisions of the Merchant Shipping Act. A yacht owner must also obtain a club certificate to show that he is a member of that particular club.

Formerly the Admiralty warrant exempted the holder from all Government dues in Great Britain; but an order came in force in 1898 by which boats of above five tons pay one shilling per ton per annum towards the maintenance of lights. The warrant entitles the yachtsman to several valuable privileges, while still further favours are extended to him as a matter of courtesy. He may, for example, use man-of-war moorings if these are not required at the time for Government purposes. When he cruises abroad, the production of his warrant will free him from all such harbour and other dues as are paid by merchantmen, but not by men-of-war. In some parts of the world, in Brazil for example, a warrant is almost indispensable; for a yacht unprovided with it would be treated as if she were a merchantman, and her owner would be put to considerable inconvenience. When the author called at Bahia with his eighteen-ton yacht the *Falcon*, his Admiralty warrant ensured him the most courteous treatment on the part of the authorities. His vessel was accorded man-of-war rights; permission was given him to anchor in the man-of-war ground instead of in the crowded mercantile anchorage, and he was permitted to go off in his boat to the yacht, or to land at the arsenal steps, at any hour of the day or night, the sentries having received instructions always to open the gates and let him through. Now the skipper of a merchantman cannot, or at any rate could not in those days, leave his vessel or go on board of her after 8 p. m., without a special licence from the Customs House, which I understand was not readily granted. Another very vexatious rule was held not to apply to me. I was not compelled, as was every merchantman, to have an insolent negro guard placed on board my vessel during my stay.

The Customs authorities abroad, in short, respect our Admiralty warrant; they relax their rules in favour of the yachtsman, are not ever suspiciously on the watch to see that he does not smuggle or otherwise break the laws of the country. He is trusted as a gentleman, and he is on his honour to observe the obligations on the strength of which the warrant was granted. The privilege should never be abused.

Registration is not compulsory for vessels of fifteen tons and under. But even a small yacht, if she is intended for foreign cruising, should be registered. In the first place, the Admiralty will not grant a warrant to an unregistered boat. The register is the most important of the ship's papers. It is a certificate of ownership granted by the Registrar-General of Shipping, and it is a ship's passport which serves to identify her and to establish her nationality when abroad. It is on her registered tonnage that a yacht has to pay harbour, light, canal, and other dues, at so much a ton. If, for example, one is sailing on the Dutch canals, the production of the register will settle beyond dispute the amount that can be rightly claimed for canal dues. But if a boat be unprovided with a register, her owner is likely to be occasionally worried by the red tape of foreign officialdom, and he will probably be made to pay dues calculated on her yacht measurement – that is, about twice as much as he should pay; for a vessel's tonnage by yacht measurement is as a rule nearly double her registered tonnage.

When the yachtsman has his boat built for him, it is a simple matter to have her registered. 'A Customs House measuring officer examines her and gives a certificate as to her tonnage, etc. This certificate, together with the builder's certificate and a declaration of ownership, are sent to the Registrar who will then grant the register. But when one purchases a second-hand unregistered vessel it often happens that one cannot trace her antecedents; and if, when applying for a register, one is unable to produce either her builder's certificate (it being unknown who built her), or her bills of sale, as the transfers from the successive owners are called, he will have to go through some formalities and be put to expense and trouble – I speak from experience – before he obtains his register.

The relations between the captain and crew of a merchantman are very clearly defined by law. But these regulations – more especially those framed for the protection of the merchant seaman – apparently do not apply to pleasure craft. The rights of the yacht sailor and the power of the yacht skipper are imperfectly understood by either party.

The yacht owner should invariably have his name inscribed on the ship's papers as her captain, even if he employ a skipper to sail his vessel for him.

The only person recognised by officials abroad as being in authority on a vessel is her captain. The owner who has his skipper entered as captain makes the latter his master, so that if the man prove unsatisfactory, and has to be discharged in a foreign harbour, it may be difficult to get rid of him, and vexatious complications may arise. Unlike the master of a merchantman, the owner of a yacht is not compelled by law to pass his examination and hold a Board of Trade certificate before he can command his vessel as captain on a foreign voyage. The Board of Trade yachting certificate is optional.

It is always well to have a written agreement with one's paid hands. Ocean cruising is beyond the scope of this work; but it may be remarked that the owner of a yacht bound on a long foreign voyage should not only be his own captain, but should make all hands – volunteers as well as paid men – sign articles in the presence of a shipping master before starting. Much future trouble may be saved by taking this precaution. Let him also religiously observe all the Board of Trade regulations as regards provisions and medicaments. An ill-conditioned sea-lawyer in his crew, on being discharged by the author in a Brazilian port, laid a complaint before the British Consul to the effect that the Board of Trade scale of provisions had not been furnished on the yacht. As a matter of fact, the scale of provisions had been far more liberal and luxurious than that specified by the Board of Trade, but in so much as it differed from it, our sea-lawyer had a technical grievance. Again, when punishing men for misconduct, only such punishments as are sanctioned by the Board of Trade must be inflicted.

Even when cruising with a small vessel, the yachtsman will do well to keep a log-book, and when he is on a foreign cruise with paid hands under him, to do so becomes imperative. For the log is the official diary in which is entered, day by day, not only the details of the ship's vogage, but the fines and other punishments inflicted on the seamen, the discharge or desertion of men, cases of death or sickness, etc.; and in case of future litigation or official inquiry the log-book has to be produced.

INSURANCE

It is now possible to insure a yacht on very easy terms with Lloyd's agents, against all risks; and it is not necessary for insurance purposes that the captain of a yacht hold a Board of Trade certificate.

In the ordinary yachting policy, clauses are inserted making the underwriters liable for a vessel's loss or partial damage to the extent of the value of the policy, whether she be at sea, in port, in dock, on a gridiron, on the mud, etc.; whether she have a pilot on board or not: in short, nearly all possible conditions are provided for, and the vessel is permitted, without invalidating her policy, to sail to any port in any part of the world.

By what is known as the collision clause, the underwriters are liable for damages inflicted by the insured yacht on some other vessel, by collision with her (even if the insured vessel be in the wrong), to the extent of three-quarters of the value of the policy.

By what is known as the average clause, the underwriters contract to pay for the repair of partial damage to the insured vessel, an average at the rate of three per cent, of the sum for which the vessel is insured.

Or by another clause, often inserted in the policies of large yachts, the underwriters are liable in full for the repair of any damage costing more than £20, but for nothing under that sum.

To cover racing risks a separate clause is inserted.

13

Two Cruises on Lateen-Rigged Craft

The following narrative will convey some idea of how the Arabs handle their somewhat clumsy, lateen-rigged craft. My dhow race in the Red Sea was sailed in the November of 1897. Military operations in the Sudan had come to a close for that season, so four correspondents and myself returned home from Berber by way of Suakin, a desert journey of 245 miles. Riding on camels and accompanied by half a dozen armed men, we reached Suakin in eleven days. From Suakin the other correspondents returned by sea to Cairo on their way home; but my destination was the Italian colony of Erythrea, for at Suakin I found awaiting me a telegram from the paper I represented ordering me to travel without delay to Kassala, which was shortly to be handed over by the Italians to the Egyptian Government. By the direct caravan route (along which I travelled some months later), Kassala is but 280 miles from Suakin, but at that time Dervish patrols were wont to water at the wells on this road, so that I could not follow it. My only plan, therefore, was to sail to the Italian port of Massowah, 300 miles down the coast, and thence ride through Erythrea, another 300 miles, to my destination. As no steamers run between Suakin and Massowah, I was compelled to charter a native sailing-craft in order to make this voyage.

It had been blowing hard from the north for several days, and I knew that if it continued to do so I could reach Massowah in two or three days with any boat that could sail at all. I soon found the very vessel for my purpose in the harbour, a dhow of about thirty tons burden. She had two masts, carrying a large lateen sail on her foremast, and a smaller one on her mizzen.

She was undecked, but her high stern was partly covered in, forming a poop on which the helmsman stood; so that under this I could find shelter during the voyage, and make myself very fairly comfortable, despite the rats and cockroaches, and the small but very aggressive and venomous mosquitoes that swarmed in that part of the vessel. She must have brought the mosquitoes from her own country, as I had come across none in Suakin or anywhere else in the Sudan. The dhow belonged to Yembo, the port of Medina, on the opposite Arabian coast, and was sailing under the Turkish flag. She was discharging a cargo of dates which she had brought from Yembo. She carried a crew of twelve men, negroes and Arabians of the Hedjaz.

I came to terms with the Arab merchant, residing in Suakin, who represented the Turkish owners of the El Hamdi – for that was the vessel's name – and I explained to him that I wished to put to sea as soon as possible, being anxious not to waste the favouring wind; for I knew that, should it shift to the southward, a fortnight or more might be occupied in beating down the coast. The skipper, therefore, set to work to discharge the remainder of his cargo as rapidly as he could, and in a few hours the dhow was at my disposal. I put on board of her my baggage and provisions for the voyage – biscuits, tinned meats, coffee, and whisky, and some goat-skins full of water – and in the afternoon the dhow dropped two miles down the reef-bound channel in order to take on board some sand from the banks as ballast, for she carried no cargo. It was arranged that I should pull off to the vessel in a shore boat at night, and that we should sail as soon as the tide served. I had been informed that another dhow, with a correspondent on board (not one of my companions on the ride from Berber, but another who had recently arrived from Cairo), had sailed that morning for Massowah, and that the said correspondent had determined to get there before me. But my skipper was proud of his vessel, and was keen to prove her qualities in a race. 'I know that they intend to do their best on the other dhow,' he said; 'but I will guarantee that, despite their long start, we will be the first to reach Massowah.'

At midnight I got a boat to take me off to the dhow. It was now blowing a full gale from the north, the sky was overcast, and it was very dark. The skipper did not like the look of the weather, and told me that he would not venture to navigate his craft on such a night among the intricate coral reefs which lie outside Suakin; and after glancing at a chart which I had brought with me, I had to acknowledge that he was right. The steamer *Southend,* on which my four colleagues had taken passage, was to have sailed that afternoon for Suez, but had postponed her departure on account of the heavy weather; so there was a good excuse for the skipper of our little open craft remaining at this safe anchorage until the morning.

The following day, November the 14th, broke wildly; the clouds were rushing across the sky, the gale was howling through our rigging, and the dhow was tumbling about and straining uneasily at her anchor. But my skipper was no timid mariner. On the contrary, like most of these fatalistic, happy-go-lucky Mussulman sailor-men, of whom so many are lost each year in these treacherous and stormy Red Sea waters, he was perhaps what Europeans would have called foolhardy; to put it more correctly, he placed more faith in Kismet than in the barometer. So, at the first appearance of light in the east, the skipper roused his men; the anchor was weighed; the great foresail was hoisted, to an Arab chanty lustily shouted; the vessel listed for a moment until the water was running over her lee-side into her hold, righted herself, and then was off like a greyhound through the smooth water inside the reef. 'The other dhow has had twenty-four hours' start,' I remarked. 'What of that?' replied the skipper. 'She, too, I know, must have been lying at anchor somewhere within the reef. We shall be at Massowah before her if we sail the *El Hamdi* as we should.' A race is always interesting, so I encouraged the crew by a promise of backshish if our dhow proved the winner, with the result that the skipper and his willing men threw themselves heartily into the sport of the thing; and had they been (as most probably some of them had been in their time) cracking on with a cargo of slaves on board to escape a pursuing British cruiser, they could not have sailed their craft more smartly. It reminded me agreeably of former yachting days; and I well knew that, should my friend on the other dhow catch sight of us, he would do his utmost to make his crew win the race. I afterwards found that this had been indeed the case.

I soon discovered that the crew of my dhow were a fine, cheery lot of men; and excellent sailors. It was a picturesque crew, too, as if it had just come out of *The Arabian Nights*; it might well have sailed under the adventurous Sindbad himself. The skipper was a jovial, old, one-eyed mariner from Jiddah; his mate was a huge fellow, black as coal, but with aquiline Arab features. The men knew their work thoroughly – were prompt in repeating each word of command and in obeying it; discipline was well maintained, and I was astonished to find how well ordered everything can be on an Arab dhow. The diet of the crew was simple and excellent; they ate their fill of dates and rice, and hospitably brought me dishes of their food at each repast. They were very regular at their morning and evening devotions; the skipper called them together at the proper hours, and himself chanted in a rather fine voice; for, being natives of Jiddah and Yembo, the ports of the two holiest cities, Mecca and Medina, they were the most fanatical of Mussulmans. One would always get on very well with these fine sailors of Arabia were it not for the fierce fanaticism lurking in their souls, ever ready to burst out, and maintaining such an impassable gulf between them and the Franks.

We soon got outside the sheltering Suakin reef, and found a heavy sea running, in which we rolled and plunged violently, occasionally shipping a good deal of water over our low sides, so that it became necessary to keep the hands constantly at the pumps. This operation was effected in a primitive fashion on board the *El Hamdi*. Pumps indeed there were none; a trough formed of a hollowed palm-tree was fastened across the vessel's waist transversely, its ends overlapping either bulwark. At the bottom of the vessel amidships was a square well, boarded in to prevent the sand ballast from falling into it. In this well stood one of the hands, knee-deep in water, filling goat-skin buckets from it as fast as he was able, and handing these out to a hand above, who, in his turn, emptied them into the trough, whence the water poured overboard from one side or the other as the vessel rolled; a slow and happy-go-lucky progress, indeed, by which it would have been impossible to bale out the dhow had we shipped a really heavy sea into our open hold.

We were running before a steep following sea, but there was but small chance of our being pooped; for like European vessels of the eighteenth century and earlier (whose lines above water were indeed very similar to those of the Arab dhow), we had a towering poop that no wave ever reached, though we had comparatively low bows and little freeboard amidships. I occasionally stood on this poop and took a spell at the helm, and I found that she steered very easily, showing no tendency to broach to. The skipper had the true racing spirit, and did not miss a chance. On the contrary, he was too ready to run considerable risks in his attempts to cut corners so as to shorten his passage or to cheat an opposing current. For example, he once took us over shoal water at the edge of some of the reefs, and the white coral was visible but a few feet beneath our keel. Here the sea became dangerously steep; there were rollers such as one sees on the weather edge of the Doggerbank in an autumn gale. The water poured over our sides in alarming volumes; the men at the baling apparatus could not keep it under; the loose sand that formed our ballast was converted into sludge, and shifted with each roll of the vessel. We were certainly, for a short time, in some danger of foundering; and this the skipper realised, for, shouting orders mingled with invocations to Allah and the Prophet, he promptly hauled his wind and made for the open sea and deeper water.

The skipper pressed the dhow under as much canvas as she could safely carry, and we had a few accidents on the way. First we sprang our heavy foreyard at the juncture of the two spars of which it was formed; so the sail was lowered and we

ran on more comfortably, but at a much reduced rate, under
the smaller mizzen, which had not yet been set, and which was
now brought forward and hoisted on the foremast. Next, with a
loud report, the sheet carried away in a squall, and the sail was
split in various places before it could be secured and got down.
We had now, therefore, to run under bare poles for a short
time, until the foresail-yard was repaired. This was done very
smartly – for Arab sailors have plenty of practice in patching
up their invariably rickety spars and gear – up went our big
foresail again, and we rushed over the seas at our former rate.
Every now and again we had to jibe – a formidable operation
in such weather with this huge lateen, which, like the English
lugsail, has to be dipped and passed over to the other side at
each jibe or tack.

At midday we were sailing in smoother water inside a
long coral reef, which extends for many miles parallel to the
coast, and forms a sheltered channel for small craft. It was
only occasionally, when we passed the openings in the reef,
that we were exposed to the heavy sea that was still running.
Later in the afternoon we sailed past the southern end of this
reef, and were again rolling and pitching merrily as we ran
before the high steep seas. Then we doubled the cape called
Ras Asis, which is about seventy miles from Suakin. From here
the coast trends, for ten miles, to the west of south, so afforded
us some shelter, the wind being from the N.N.W. At about
sunset the skipper lowered his sail and let go his anchor close
under the shore, which was low and barren, and appeared to be
uninhabited. He explained to me – and my chart confirmed his
words – that there was no safe anchorage further on with this
wind blowing, and that the numerous islets and shoals, among
which we had to pick our way, rendered navigation dangerous
on a dark night. But the skipper was still confident that, despite
this delay, we should overhaul our adversary on the morrow. He
knew that he was no less daring than the master of the other
dhow, and that the latter would come to an anchor at least as
often as he did.

We rolled about a good deal that night, and before dawn on November 15 the skipper roused his sleeping crew, who promptly went to their work in their fluttering white robes, singing their chanties as usual while they got up anchor and sail. The wind was now moderating, and soon it fell light, and the rain began to fall. We travelled slowly over an oily swell, our sail flapping with every roll. Now and again, however, a short but violent squall swept down upon us and drove the dhow hissing through the water for a while. At about nine o'clock in the morning we sighted two craft ahead of us. We soon distinguished them as being two-masted dhows, one coming our way and the other apparently sailing the same course as ourselves. 'That one,' said the skipper, 'is the felucca with the Englishman on board. We are now certain to be in port before her. The *El Hamdi* can sail; the other cannot.'

The crew now spared no effort to overtake the chase; as there were no longer squalls of dangerous violence, they, for the first time, cracked on all the canvas they could. From a sack they produced a sail I had not yet seen, which proved to be a large foresail of light canvas, intended for use only in moderate breezes, and possibly in case of pursuit when the vessel was engaged in contraband trade. The head of the foresail, under which we had been sailing so far, was ten feet shorter than the yard on which it was bent; but when this was lowered and the new foresail was bent on in its place, I saw that the head of the latter extended from end to end of the spar, and that this sail was also considerably longer along the foot, so that we were now spreading a very large area of canvas. The mizzen, which had been repaired, was also hoisted, and the watchful skipper carefully trimmed his sheets to each shift of the variable breeze. Whenever possible, we sailed with our lateens goose-winged.

We passed close to the dhow that was tacking towards us; and her *reis,* when we hailed him, confirmed what our skipper had said. 'There is a Feringhi on the vessel ahead,' he shouted. The sky cleared, and our crew were employed in drying their drenched garments, as we sailed very slowly on before the gradually failing wind; but all the while we gained steadily on the other dhow, and at one o'clock we were about two miles astern of her. Then it fell calm for a few hours, and our sails hung uselessly flapping and chafing from the groaning yards as we wallowed in the swell. An hour before sunset a light breeze sprang up from the south of east, so that our tacks were brought amidship and our sheets were flattened in; for we could just lay our course close-hauled on the port tack. The wind soon freshened, and we began to overhaul our adversary rapidly. Shortly after dark a squall struck us. The *El Hamdi* proved herself very fast on a wind : leaning well over, with the water rippling over her lee bulwarks, we shot by the other dhow as if she were standing still; and in a few minutes left her astern, out of sight in the growing darkness, for these happy-go-lucky dhows but rarely carry lights at night.

Then my proud and delighted skipper came up and shook hands with me heartily, and the crew hurried aft to congratulate me after the true Arab fashion. Discipline was cast aside for the nonce. The gigantic black mate at the helm alone took charge of the ship. The others expressed their triumph by the Arab *fantasia* of victory. A lantern was hung up, a tom-tom and stringed instruments were produced, and while four of the men squatted in front of me and played with furious energy on these instruments, the rest wildly danced and shouted and clapped their hands. This orgy lasted for several hours; and when they wearied, the men enjoyed the luxurious supper that had been provided for them, consisting of rice to eat, water to drink, and some tobacco, which I had given them to smoke. It was a celebration of victory that would have astonished a winning crew at Cowes.

We did not come to an anchor this night, as the coast was now clear, with no outlying reefs or shoals to pick us up. Our black mate was at the helm all night; for the steering had now to be done by compass, and he was the only one of the crew who understood the English box-compass he had with him on the poop, and of which he was inordinately proud. He was very interested in my chart, and evidently comprehended it thoroughly, when I read the names out to him and pointed out the various landmarks. We made good way till dawn, when we had the low desert mainland close to us on our starboard hand, and over our port-bow the island of Difnein, on which there is a lighthouse, seventy miles from Massowah. We sailed before light breezes through the smooth green water, and at four in the afternoon were abreast of the south end of Harat Island, where there is another light, and but twenty-five miles from our destination.

The wind now headed us, and freshened considerably. We took long tacks, and sailed, with all possible canvas set, our lee bulwarks nearly level with the water. So soon as the sun was down we sighted the lights of Massowah, and at seven o'clock we came to an anchor outside the harbour, awaiting daylight to get in. We had thus made the voyage in a little over sixty hours, which was fair work considering the light breezes and calms we had encountered for a portion of the way. Early on the following morning we sailed into the spacious harbour, let go our anchor, and hoisted the Turkish ensign. As soon as we had got pratique I bade farewell to my friendly skipper and his crew, and put off to the quay in the dhow's boat. Shortly afterwards I saw the other dhow (which had been sailing through the night while we lay at anchor) come in. My friend had done his utmost to urge on his crew, and they had tried their best to outstrip us; but we had beaten them very easily, having sailed two knots to their one. Ours was the larger and faster vessel, and I think we carried the better crew. My dhow sailed for Jiddah that afternoon, while I, turning my back on the sea for awhile, travelled inland on mules and camels across six hundred miles of mountain and desert.

The voyage I am now about to describe is very different from that I undertook in the Red Sea on the dhow *El Hamdi*. To any who contemplate the navigation, with a sailing craft, of the rapids of a great river, the following narrative may afford some useful hints.

It was in October 1896. I had been representing the *Times* in the Sudan. For seven months, throughout an exceptionally torrid summer, even for the Sudan, the Nile expeditionary force had been marching, fighting, or sweltering in desert cholera camps; the battles of Firket and Hafir had been fought; Dongola and Merawi had been occupied; five hundred miles of the Nile Valley had been recovered from the Dervish tyranny; the campaign had come to a close for that year, and it was known that the Egyptian army would make no further advance until the following summer.

We war correspondents sold our horses and camels, and made arrangements to travel down the Nile by boat from Dongola to Kosheh, which was at that time the southern terminus of the military railway. Permission was given to us to take passage on the Government sailing-boats, of which many were employed in transporting supplies from Kosheh to the southern garrisons. On 30 September a strong wind brought up to Dongola a large fleet of *gayassas,* which were promptly unloaded and despatched back to Kosheh for further cargoes. A big two-masted boat was placed at the disposal of myself and the correspondent of another paper. She was fifty feet in length and fourteen in breadth, and carried two large lateen sails. Her *reis* and his crew of two lazy Berberis were from the north, and knew but little of this portion of the river; but happily we had with us one of my camel-drivers, an old man called Oshea (an Arab and not an Irishman, as one would imagine from his name), who was a native of the Dongola province, and was able to direct the *reis* in the intricate navigation of the rock-encumbered rapids. On the evening of September 30th we embarked with our servants and an Egyptian soldier, whose duty it was to accompany the *gayassa* on her voyage, and prevent the lazy crew from lingering too long on the way.

It was an interesting journey, for we frequently landed on the river-bank, or on the green islands, and had an opportunity of observing the immediate results of the reoccupation of the province by the Egyptians. The people seemed contented, and showed complete confidence in the first Europeans they had seen for many years. They were evidently pleased to be rid of the

Dervish yoke, and had already resumed the cultivation of the land; where-ever the Dervishes had left any oxen to turn the waterwheels, we heard the droning of the *sakiyehs* as they raised the water from the river to irrigate the fields. Though we had a strong stream under us, the voyage from Dongola to Kosheh, a distance of about 200 miles, occupied nearly six days; and our soldiers told us that the boat on her last voyage had taken no less than fifteen days to sail up the river from Kosheh to Dongola. Our progress would have been even slower than it was had we not constantly stirred up the lazy *reis,* who was of the opinion that the proper way to take a boat down the river was to let her drift idly all day and tie her up to the bank each night, so that he could enjoy his eight hours' slumber. As at this season the north wind generally blows hard throughout the day to impede a boat's drifting, whereas at night it is calm, we compelled the old man to continue his navigation throughout a great portion of the night, except when we were on dangerous portions of the river.

The men seldom use their oars on these larger *gayassas,* and guide the clumsy flat-bottomed craft down-stream after the following fashion. If the north breeze blows hard against the current, the head of the vessel is turned up-stream, and as the empty boat draws little water, and her high prow exposes a large surface to hold the wind, good steerage-way is gained, which enables the *reis* to keep her in the strength of the current and to avoid dangers. The result is that one is often travelling through the water at quite two knots in the direction opposite to that in which one is bound, though at the same time the favouring stream running four knots under the vessel enables one to make progress northward at the rate of two knots an hour. Sometimes, again, when the wind was light, and he required more steerage-way in order to dodge the shallows and rocks, over which the river rushed with an ominous roar, the *reis* hoisted his foresail, or, if necessary, both his sails. Occasionally, too, he tacked backwards and forwards across the river; and it was then, I think, that our progress was slowest, for the leeway made by that *gayassa* was extraordinary; and, as she would not go about, the *reis* had to wear her each time – an operation which involved running fast up-stream before the wind for fully five minutes, before the clumsy craft, after jibing, would luff up and sail close-hauled again on the other tack. It was a curious and paradoxical style of navigation. The faster we wished to travel the less sail we carried, and we were at our best under bare poles or in a dead calm. It was only at the approach of danger that our prudent skipper hoisted all his canvas, and it was only when a clear channel was before him that he boldly furled both his sails and allowed his craft to rush madly down the stream. For thousands of years the indolent Nile mariners have been content with this leisurely navigation; and yet it would be easy, by fitting leeboards on one of these craft, to enable her to accomplish the downward voyage in less than half the time now occupied, for at high Nile the river is generally broad and unobstructed by rocks, so that a vessel could tack down boldly between bank and bank; it is only at the cataracts that caution has to be observed.

But, slow as it was, our voyage was an enjoyable one. After our long marches across the dreary deserts it was pleasant to get away from the dust-storm and the fiery heat, and float lazily down the broad stream. The country on either side looked wonderfully green and fertile to us; for from the water we could not see the barren sands that stretched beyond the narrow belts of cultivation. We drifted between palm-groves, pastures, and fields of tall maize, past many villages and groaning waterwheels, and it was difficult for us to realise that the fair shore was but a thin mask in front of the world's most hopeless and hideous wildernesses. Now we were winding through archipelagoes of verdant islands, and now descending long reaches two miles in breadth, where our vessel tossed on the muddy waves raised by the conflicting wind and tide. We skirted the fertile island of Argo, which is twenty-five miles in length. We landed at several villages on this island in order to purchase fowls, which the inhabitants, though well disposed to us, were unwilling to sell, as they have little use for money. Here, too, we saw some large *gayassas* in course of construction on the shore; for Argo is famous throughout the Sudan as a great shipbuilding centre. The Mahdi's family came from Argo, and were known for many generations as expert boat-builders. The timbers and knees of these craft are of the hard wood of the native acacia, while the masts and planking are of imported Norwegian pine; how this was procured while the Dervishes closed the Sudan to trade it is difficult to say.

There were plenty of sailing craft on the river. Some, downward bound, performing the same clumsy evolutions as our own, a few of them crowded with Dervish prisoners, still clad in the Mahdist patched *jibbas* and turbans, on their way to Haifa; others upward bound, deeply laden with supplies for our troops, rushing through the water under their great lateens, the two-masted boats with their sails goosewinged. On October 2nd we passed Hafir and the scene of our recent fight. Then we shot the Hannek, or Third Cataract of the Nile, at that season a long series of rapids, through which we threaded our devious way between innumerable rocks and whirlpools. We were more fortunate than two other correspondents who had preceded us, and who had capsized here, lost their kits, and drifted several hours down the rapids, holding on to the bottom of the overturned and often submerged boat.

It was now, amid these really dangerous rapids, when a slight error of judgment would have brought instant shipwreck and probable loss of life, that our old *reis* showed that he knew his work after all. His lazy expression vanished; his eye keenly scanned the broken water round him as he firmly held the tiller and shouted his orders as to the handling of the sails to the two lads. Generally with the head of his vessel pointing up-stream and foresail set to give him good steerage-way, he cleverly guided the boat, so that, well in hand, she drifted stern foremost between the numerous dangers, rocks always close to him on either side and angry whirlpools ever and anon rising at his bows as if with intent to throw the *gayassa* off hef course, and dash her on the treacherous needles of rock that lay in wait beneath the foaming water. Sometimes he sailed across the river to seek the safest channel through a rocky reef; having found it, he placed his boat in mid-entrance of it, and then, having done all that lay in his power, he loudly invoked the assistance of Allah, and left her to be swept helplessly down the boiling rapid, escaping destruction by but a few yards on either hand. Sometimes, when he perceived no serious difficulties ahead, he triced up his sail to allow the boat to drift the faster; on the other hand, when approaching an exceptionally dangerous bit of water, he carried mainsail as well as foresail, so that the vessel remained practically stationary, the wind pressure just counteracting the influence of the current; and he was thus enabled to scan the broken water below him at leisure, select his road, and form his plan of action, before reducing canvas again and allowing the boat to be carried down. The old *reis* rose in my estimation; for though, when in safe reaches of the river, lazy, awkward in the handling of his boat, frequently running into the bank, or grounding on a shoal through sheer carelessness, he was always, when put on his mettle by the perils of a cataract, the able skipper, prompt in action, possessing unerring judgment and iron nerve. When descending a cataract it is, of course, always well to have a contrary wind, as was the case that day. When a south wind combines with the torrent to drive a vessel through these rock-sown rapids, the most skilful *reis* can have but little control over her course, and it must be by good luck chiefly that disaster is avoided.

In the evening of the same day we came to the ruins of an old Roman fort, crowning a height on the left bank. Here the channel is much narrowed, being hemmed in by rocky bluffs. The Nile, pouring through this defile, is dashed into a wild confusion of breakers, whirlpools, and shifting eddies. It was an extraordinary and ever-changing spectacle. The water boiled and roared around us as in a violent tide-race at sea. In the midst of a still piece of water a whirlpool would suddenly form; gyrating with ever-increasing velocity, it would yawn wider and wider, as if preparing to swallow up our vessel, and then disappear as suddenly as it had arisen. Next a streak of foaming water would shoot hissing athwart the channel, as if it were some javelin hurled at us by the angry river spirit, strike our vessel on bow or stern, and whirl her round like a teetotum. Near the banks the water was almost still, but we found it impossible to creep up along them and so pass the central eddies, for a strong undertow always sucked us out into the vortex. In this strange place we remained quite an hour without making any progress, buffeted by the steep waves and the whirlpools, often revolving dizzily, while round and round us ever seemed to spin the ruined Roman castle on the hill. Sometimes we contrived to steal down to the lower end of this race, but then, even as if the jinn of the whirlpool were playing with their captives, up would spring some sudden malicious counter-current to sweep us back again to our former position. It was just such an enchanted piece of water as one reads of in the old fairy tales, from which the hapless mariner can never effect his escape once his vessel has been drawn within the magic circle. Oshea, who knew these narrows well, told us that boats were sometimes kept tossing about here for three days or more before they could get through. We were more fortunate; for suddenly, I know not how, our boat shot out of the uncanny gulf, and we drifted away.

On October the 3rd we went down the Kaibar cataract, which presents no serious difficulties, and on the 4th reached the large village of Kub-el-Selim on the west bank, a thriving-looking settlement surrounded by great groves of date-palms. This was the country of Oshea, and he was to leave our service here, so we put him on shore. He insisted on taking us to see his house. I now realised that our camel-driver was a man of considerable importance when at home. He was a member of the chief family of the place, and his brother was sheikh of the village. Oshea owned many date-trees and cattle. He possessed a spacious house of many chambers, wherein dwelt his wife and children. He had a second wife at some place further north, and told us that he now intended, despite his years, to invest a portion of the wages he had received from us in the purchase of yet a third and younger wife, for whom he intended to set up an establishment in Dongola. He would thus never be far removed from some home and family during his wanderings up and down the Nile. Hospitable as behoves an Arab, Oshea regaled us with coffee, cakes, and dates from his own palm-groves, and gave us a fat sheep to take on board with us.

On October the 5th we reached Kosheh, delivered the *gayassa* to the authorities, and travelled to Cairo by train and steamer.

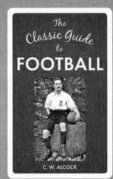